Foreword

The sketches in the LONDON and SARANAC LAKE sections are arranged more or less according to when each was written. The NEW YORK CITY pieces are arranged thematically; the dates represent alternately the time of writing or the time in which they are set. The essays in SUNDAY MATTERS are not pegged to dates.

Many have been previously published at *www.Geezerblockhead.com.*

In Passing. Scenes from an Unconventional Life

PAUL WILLCOTT

Published by Wordstruck Press, 2024.

While every precaution has been taken in the preparation of this book, the publisher assumes no responsibility for errors or omissions, or for damages resulting from the use of the information contained herein.

IN PASSING. SCENES FROM AN UNCONVENTIONAL LIFE

First edition. December 2, 2024.

Copyright © 2024 PAUL WILLCOTT.

ISBN: 979-8227576811

Written by PAUL WILLCOTT.

Also by PAUL WILLCOTT

Annals of Franklin Manor
A Franklin Manor Christmas
A Franklin Manor Epiphany

Standalone
12,000 Miles of Road Thoughts. Old Van, Old Man, Recovering Hippie, Dying Cat
In Passing. Scenes from an Unconventional Life

Watch for more at paulwillcott.com.

Table of Contents

Preface 1
London 3
Peewee | 1987-2001 5
Trailing Spouse | 1993 13
Spring Comes to London | 1993 17
Hockney, the Brontes, and the Yorkshire Dales | 1993 23
Remembering War | 1994 29
New York City 33
Lapsed Texan | 2003 35
W, Recovering Divider | 2002 39
Upper West Side | 1996 41
Home Again – in Brooklyn | 1998 45
The Great Saunter | 1999 47
Bronx Hardware Store | 1999 53
Moving as Dying | 2014 59
That Feeling-at-Home Feeling | 2021 69
My River | 2022 73
Adirondacks 75
A Powerful House | 1999 77
Pell, Bill Gruber, and the Flag | 2001 81
Finally, a Big Christmas Tree | 2003 85
The Trouble with My Porch Swing | 2004 93
Winter Nights in the Monastery | 2016 105
Frame of Reference | 2016 111
Sunday Matters 119
Bananas 121
Empty Pews. Why They Should Matter to Everyone 125
Sundays There and Here, Then and Now 131

Preface

"One thing a writer can do is create a world into which the reader can slip for just a while and think it would be pleasant to stay. That's what Willcott does."

National Society of Newspaper Columnists Award

London

Peewee
1987-2001

It's quite confusing is Cherry Trees International Quarantine and Boarding Cattery – part reformatory, part progressive school. The poor babies never know whether it's going to be thin soup and cold showers or pampering and teatime.

Cherry Trees is used by people who bring cats into England. Six months at Cherry Trees will satisfy Her Majesty's veterinarian that they are not rabid and have earned the right to pass from maximum security into Britain at large. Query: will there be a graduation ceremony at the end, or will Tabby just get the kitty equivalent of a new suit and some pocket change along with the warden's admonition to be careful out there?

The four concrete-block buildings are laid out in connecting wings like cell blocks. Each room has a window reinforced with heavy steel mesh, but there are curtains, and at every curtained window, a cat peers out. Some stare blankly, long since having given in to despair. Others beg and cry, their mouths opening soundlessly behind their windows.

Visiting is permitted for two hours on Saturday afternoons and at other times by special arrangement. Two rules govern visits. One must phone ahead – no drop-in visits allowed. The mind leaps seeking possible reasons for this practice. Do the operators of the cattery groom Tabby between phone call and arrival? A place that has little kitty curtains in the little kitty windows just might. And perhaps a modest hit of kitty mood elevators is administered before Mom and Dad arrive? Can't have Tabby looking blue during visiting hours. Kitty stiff upper lip, that sort of thing

The second visiting rule is that if Tabby is upset by a visit, subsequent visits will not be permitted. The temptation is great to ask how Tabby manifests this emotional state.

Visitors enter the compound though a single door, which is kept locked. Upon admission, one signs in, and then an attendant leads the way through two more locked doors. Tabby's room also has a locked door, lest some distressed owner, made crazy by the prospect of six months without Tabby, tries to break her out before her time has been served.

"How long would you like to stay?" the attendant asks. Upon receiving an answer, he leaves, locking all doors behind him. At that point, Tabby, Mom, and Dad have four locked doors between them and the outside. The prison vision begins to overwhelm that of progressive school.

Each 5 x 5 room has a plastic stool, a large shelf under the window, a kitty bed on the shelf, and a heat lamp over the bed. All in all, not unlike a New York "frnshd eff. w. loft; great charm." The bill for the electricity that runs the heat lamp allays any worry about Tabby being chilly.

The wall on the hall side is made of heavy steel mesh, which enables each resident to communicate with the other eight or ten on the wing. One wonders if they swap contraband. And who decides what they listen to on the one radio that plays constantly? Probably Bruno, the big tom in Number Three.

In addition to the standard-issue furniture, each room is personalized with toys and favorite blankets and such. One expects to see snapshots of the old lady and girlie calendars.

Visitors spend their time in various ways – reading, napping on the floor, and talking inanities to Tabby. A couple of hours in a spartan 5 x 5 room with a cat may seem like a long time, especially if one doesn't enjoy Nat King Cole (Bruno's favorite), but one can always speed the time trying to picture in the mind the person down the hall who is overheard cooing, "Oh, did Puss make poopy? Oooh, good kitty."

At the end of visiting hours, guests file down the narrow halls amid much unlocking and relocking of doors, all the while wondering if the afternoon's activities have been consistent with human dignity. Upon reaching the office near the outermost door, leftover Good Girl Goodies (a treat sold by the cattery) and kitty toothbrushes are turned in for safekeeping until the next visit.

When the last visitor leaves, the outer door is locked, and kitty tea is served.

Posh as Cherry Trees International Quarantine and Boarding Cattery was, our Peewee didn't like it. When we visited, he would greet us with yowling that was equal parts welcome and complaint. That was not especially remarkable. Many cats might have done that – but it started almost as soon as we got out of our car – before, it would seem, he could possibly have known we were on the premises. His wailing grew louder and filled his wing when we passed through the first of the three locked doors and began walking the long narrow hall toward his apartment. That was Peewee.

Some years before we moved to London and were living in Austin, I came down with a respiratory infection accompanied by fever and painful ulcers in my throat. Drugs offered little relief, and they made me confused. (The closest I could get to recalling the Twenty-third Psalm was, "The Lord is my shepherd, I cannot walk.") For several days, I slept little; every time I nodded off, the sharp pain from involuntary swallowing would startle me awake.

After several days of this, Peewee, then quite young, performed the first of a lifetime of mysterious feats. He got on my chest, looked into my eyes, and purring a rumbling incantation, put his paws on each side of my throat. My fever broke and the pain eased and I slept.

His laying on of paws followed an ancient practice, though one performed presumably only by humans. (Peewee was not one to let that stand in his way.) Christian confirmation, ordination, and healing rites all involve laying on of hands. In Hebrew history, Moses passed his authority as leader of the Israelites to Joshua by laying on of hands. In every instance, the recipient is fundamentally changed. Joshua, for example, became "full of the spirit of wisdom."

Peewee's blessing did something like that for me. It made me forever certain of two things that I'd not thought much about before then: some experience is beyond human understanding, and the bright-line distinction most humans draw between themselves and other animals is open to question. Not only that, but since deliverance from pain can arrive unbidden through the paws of a foundling cat, perhaps Ann and I were worrying too much about our finances.

Some background.

Peewee was a longhaired tabby of unknown lineage. He was waiting for Ann at a bus stop one day in 1987. He seemed too young to be away from his mother, and the street was choked with traffic. It was a dangerous place for a kitten to be.

Alarmed by street noises, he was performing jack-in-the-box moves as Ann stepped down from the bus. She watched him do this once, maybe twice – I'm sure not more than that – before she said, "OK, one saucer of milk." If we hadn't already had several cats, she would not have pretended he wasn't coming to stay.

This occurred when our circumstances were such that we were struggling not to be overcome by anxiety.

I was forty-nine years old and still trying to figure out what I wanted to be when I grew up. I had a Ph.D., and I'd taught English and linguistics for a few years until I realized that I was more dilettante than scholar and that being a college professor of the sort I wanted to be required being a scholar. That and certain disagreeable aspects of the work led me to resign abruptly just before the start of classes one autumn. That was followed by years of looking for a calling or at least a more suitable way to make a living.

IN PASSING. SCENES FROM AN UNCONVENTIONAL LIFE

When Ann and I married in 1985, I was unhappily teaching a course at the local community college while doing a fine job of failing as a real estate broker. Even if I had been willing, the door to full-time, tenure-track teaching had closed and was locked. Ann, almost a generation younger than I, was looking for something other than part-time work as a baker and graduate study in film history and criticism. She was passionate about her studies, but it was leading only to college teaching, a prospect she, like I, had no interest in.

Our financial future was bleak. So after a time, Ann enrolled in law school. She enjoyed it so much, she suggested that I, too, go to law school. Sure. Why not? We borrowed money to live on, and a month before my fiftieth birthday, I lined up with a bunch of twenty-somethings, tried to ignore their stares, and filed into class. I mostly enjoyed the experience and benefited from it, but early on, I realized my heart was not in the practice of law any more than it had been in anything else I had tried. I stuck it out, though, till I became a member of the New York Bar, from which I resigned almost immediately and resumed my search for fulfilling work.

When Ann brought Peewee home from the bus stop, she was in law school. We were so broke that one day we emptied our piggy bank and raced to deposit the coins to keep a check from bouncing. We bought day-old bread at a commercial bakery outlet. It was during that frightening time that Peewee healed me and started both of us thinking in a new way about the nature of reality.

Upon graduating with honors, Ann accepted a position with a prestigious Wall Street firm. I had another semester or so to complete in Austin, so she moved to New York without me.

There was never any question about what to do with the cats. We found Austin homes for Tom, Whitey Bear, and Clorox. Peewee went to New York with Ann. She judged Brooklyn streets to be too tough for him, so he had to learn to be an indoor cat. He disliked that, and he made his dislike clear. The first time Ann left him in her apartment while she was at work, he pooped under the bed covers. He did the same on the second day. On the third, Ann locked him in the bathroom with a litter box. When she returned after a twelve-hour day, the litter box was empty, and he went straight to the bed. Ann brought the contest to an end with *words,* which, true to form, he understood. She said – with some force, I imagine – "If this is going to be a contest, *I'm going to win."* He conceded.

Peewee was no less an angel in this episode than he had been in the laying on of paws. It was just that for a few days, he was a fallen angel. Such a reversion happened many times over the years. He peed in the open suitcase of some guests he didn't like. He slipped out of a cabin on Moosehead Lake in Maine one snowy ten-below night and led us on an unsuccessful tracking adventure returning on his own after we had given him up for lost. On a Sunday afternoon years later, he holed up in an inaccessible place among floor joists of a vacation home and postponed for several hours our return to New York City.

After a couple of years in New York, Ann transferred to the firm's London office. Peewee and I went with her, and Peewee served his six-month quarantine at Cherry Trees International Quarantine and Boarding Cattery.

We returned to New York after almost four years, then moved to Hong Kong for a time, again taking Peewee with us, then back to New York. At that point, we thought Ann's foreign work opportunities were finished. (They were not; several years later, we moved to Zurich.) We began trying to settle down. In the village of Saranac Lake in the Adirondack Mountains, we came across a run-down 12,000-square-foot Carmelite monastery that had previously been a tuberculosis sanatorium. After two quick walk-throughs, we bought it as a vacation getaway. It was not deconsecrated before we took ownership, and over the years, we often felt its sanctity.

Peewee enjoyed several years of weekends and holidays there, stretched full length on one of several warm hearths during the long

IN PASSING. SCENES FROM AN UNCONVENTIONAL LIFE

winters or in a breezy window during summer. Then his kidneys began to fail.

The prognosis was unequivocal; his disease was terminal. We were able to keep him alive for a time by administering subcutaneous fluid injections, but he resisted the shots, and the treatment didn't help as much as we'd hoped. When his weight dropped from thirteen pounds to six, and he began to withdraw and spend most of his time sleeping in a corner on a bare floor, we knew it was time.

Handing him over the counter at the New York City veterinarian's office, then getting his body back packed in dry ice for the trip to Saranac Lake for burial was unacceptable. A mechanical, impersonal shove into the beyond would be a betrayal.

I tried to persuade the veterinarian to give me the drug and a syringe so Ann and I could see him off personally and lovingly. It was not permitted. But we did find a way that was less unacceptable.

En route to the former monastery on a Friday evening, we phoned a vet at his home in Saranac Lake. He kindly agreed to come by, but he couldn't make it until around supper time the next day. It made for a long drive and a long day following.

People seldom lose a beloved pet without telling themselves that their cat/dog/horse/parakeet was dear and charming without qualification. Peewee was that and more; he was an angel. He revealed that early in his life, many times over in years following, and perhaps to be sure we'd gotten the point, he gave a capstone demonstration at the monastery on the last day of his life.

During the week preceding his death, he hardly ate or drank. He moved little. On the Friday-night drive up to the mountains, he lay on the back seat instead of on Ann's lap as he usually did.

When I woke on Saturday morning, I found him on the window seat in the parlor. He yawned, meowed, and stretched his paws up to me as he had on almost every morning of his life. I picked him up, and he rubbed his face against my shoulder and purred like he'd never felt better. I took him to Ann, who was still in bed, and he did what he always did. He curled up on her breast and purred and was as affectionate and content as a kitty could be.

We knew what he was up to; we didn't think for a moment that he had recovered. He was telling us he was reconciled. For the rest of that day of waiting for the vet, he would reprise his happy life, showing us what we should remember about him and giving us a model for how to die.

After some quiet time with Ann, he led us to the door and asked to go outside. It didn't matter that it was raining a little. His time was short, and he was not going to be deterred by rain. He sniffed the flowers and bushes and sort of walked the property line, then came up on the porch where we were waiting, sat down, and took a good long look at things.

We all went back inside, and after a bit, I lost track of him. Later, I heard a noise in the parlor and thought he must be in the throes of death. Not yet. He was jumping up trying to catch a moth, turning young-kitten type back flips, playing, and having a fine time.

Along about noon, he ran out of energy and turned to less active parts of the reprise. He made a place on Ann's lap and fell asleep purring. We watched it rain and waited for the veterinarian. Peewee looked up at Ann now and then. He put his head in my hand when I petted him. He told us quite clearly that he'd had a good life, and he was at peace. He was on Ann's lap when his breathing stopped.

He died as he lived – mysterious and sustaining, guardian and messenger.

Perhaps the way of his dying would have been the same wherever it occurred, but I don't think so. The sanatorium/monastery – space first given to care of the body, then consecrated to care of the soul – formed his last day in a way that exceeds human understanding.

Trailing Spouse
1993

A "trailing spouse" is the one who follows when the career of the other calls for relocating. Husbands who trail are unusual, and they attract attention. Generally speaking, there is a sense that something is not quite right about a marriage in which the wife accepts transfers and is the primary breadwinner and the husband embraces a role that is, in many ways, secondary and supportive. I became a trailing spouse in 1992.

To the curious and judgmental, I try to explain it, I make jokes about it, I stutter, and I'm a little embarrassed. Ann and I chose this way together, and we've had few regrets about it, but getting comfortable with it is a process. We find it difficult to shake off the traditional way of marriage; we are bullied by the ghosts of Ward and June. And our arrangement is made more peculiar by my being almost a generation older than Ann.

I've been supportive of feminism pretty much ever since it came along, though not for the usual reasons. I was born at the end of the depression into a working-class family. During my childhood, women were restricted in their career choices. So were men. Feminism has always appealed to me for the possibility of freedom that it offers both sexes.

Going to law school in middle age in hopes of finding work I could be passionate about had not worked out. There were several reasons for this. Probably the most important – I was an indifferent student. Also, I had thought I was signing up for a trade school, like learning to be a plumber. It turned out that legal education in the more prestigious institutions, such as the University of Texas, is designed to hatch and certify philosopher-kings.

So, when we moved to New York, I returned to my earlier career – teaching English – this time at a night school for paralegals. I was coming to terms with that and taking a few small steps in the direction of a satisfying career, when Ann had an opportunity to go to London with her firm. We embraced it eagerly.

I have been unable to find employment in London, I have become a more obviously trailing spouse, and I have begun to do what homemakers do. I have learned to clean house (a little), and to take pleasure in grocery shopping and cooking. To complete the transition to my new identity, I have added frustrated novelist, kitchen table variety. On the days when Ann finds her work not too onerous, there is much to recommend about our arrangement.

It is not without problems, though. Most notably, neither of us can fully accept our pattern. We don't feel quite right about it. It seems like nobody feels right about it. Friends and family ask in roundabout ways if I have found a job yet. My eighty-six-year-old, BMW-driving mother, who refuses to retire from her work, jokes (sort of) that I could probably learn to say, "Welcome to Wal-Mart." Neighbors have a hard time understanding why Ann gets dressed and leaves for work in the morning, while I hang around the apartment in my jeans.

Sometimes, when I am introduced to one of the masters of the universe Ann works with, they can find little to say to me. They treat me like a housewife or something. I try to have fun with that. To the overworked single lawyers who are too busy to pick up their laundry or balance their checkbooks, I offer to be a wife-for-hire and do those chores for them.

Men my age are expected to be at the top of some heap or other. To be otherwise is tantamount to failure. I shrug it off with a "business" card, which I made on an arcade machine at around midnight while walking home from a cheerful evening at a pub.

IN PASSING. SCENES FROM AN UNCONVENTIONAL LIFE

Paul Willcott, Ph.D., J.D.
Erstwhile professor
Attorney (not in practice)
Novelist manqué
Good credit risk

Spring Comes to London
1993

The surprise of April has once again come to London. I open the front door of my red-brick rowhouse to bring in the bottled milk, and the soft spring warmth takes me to lives I've already lived, places I've already been.

I grew up in Beaumont, Texas, which is on the Gulf Coast where hills of pine forest turn into coastal plain. Its people were squeezed in among petrochemical plants, rice fields, and lumber mills. One part of town was defined by Magnolia Refinery, with its rotten-egg smell and houses made yellow by the hydrogen sulfide and other unpleasant stuff it secreted. A short bike ride to the west, we would swim with snakes in irrigation canals. Just a little to the east or north, we would forage in the bottomland along the Neches River heavily armed with single-shot .22s and Daisy Red Ryder BB guns shooting every rusty can that crossed our path.

It seemed to rain more often than not, and rainy days meant that at school, we had to spend the waiting-for-the-bell time in the morning as well as recess and lunch hour and P.E. class inside in the basement (in grade school) or the gym (in junior high). They were filled with the smell of sweating children, and the floor-sweeping material that looked like crumbled pink erasers and the shrill echoing of the voices of dozens of school kids as they tried to dodge the ball thrown by some future major league pitcher.

On sunny days during junior high, life inside the school buildings hardly existed. We took our bodies in when required, but our real selves remained outside on "the big field," pronounced with emphasis on "big." The BIG field was a square of grass and clover on which there were two football goal posts, an old live oak ("the BIG tree") near the perimeter farthest from the school building, and a chain link fence on three sides. We never questioned why a place thirty or forty yards on a side should be called "big." In any case, it easily encompassed many dimensions of young boy lives.

Berlin Cassidy suffered a compound fracture of his femur while playing soccer out there one fine spring day. It was the first and only time most of us had ever seen bone sticking through skin.

Teeter Burge, "dec'd" young according to the high school alum letter, and Ronny Van Meter met on the BIG field one day at noon to settle some score. The fight lasted the whole lunch period and was still in full swing when the bell rang. Actually, it wasn't so much a fight as it was a set piece in which they took turns hitting each other with all their young-adolescent might. One would smash the other in the face, knocking him to the ground. Then the one on the ground would get up and return the favor. The rest of us stood around them in a circle cheering. We went back to class with Teeter and Ronny rubbing and shaking their painful hands.

Under the BIG tree, we worked on the latest tricks with our new Duncan yo-yos and passed around the porn comics called "eight-page bibles," which appeared every spring at about the same time as yo-yos. Young boys' hormones must be awfully powerful, because we sure did get stirred up by crude little drawings of Orphan Annie getting it on with Daddy Warbucks. For weeks after, you could always get a laugh by saying "arf."

Hardly anyone wore shoes to school in warm weather. Mary Ann, who was said to live on a river boat somewhere over by the refinery, was poorer than the rest of us. She seldom wore shoes in any weather, and we made fun of her unmercifully. Mr. Smith, the principal, told us to stop, but we didn't.

Even those who usually did wear shoes abandoned them when April brought clover up on the BIG field. Smelling its little blossoms and looking at the new green color was not enough. It seems we could only apprehend the miracle of spring by feeling the new clover with our bare feet. And as soon as we felt it, we were compelled to see how fast we could run, how far we could throw, and how high we could jump. I see BIG-field clover by the milk on the springtime doorstep of my London flat.

A sunny April morning in London – they do occur now and then – is often hazy. Coal is not used to heat houses here anymore, but there are far too many cars, and the catalytic converter has only recently made its appearance. But never mind. It looks pretty much like a fine morning in Beaumont. I am in another time and place before I realize that the shroud over my lovely back garden in London is polluted air, not mist rising over an East Texas lake teeming with white bass.

The windows across the back bedroom extend from my knees to a little higher than I can reach. They overlook the gardens that are behind all the houses on our side of the street as well as those from the other side of the block. Below the windows are layer on layer of blooming growth.

Almost within arm's reach is a bright yellow forsythia of unusual size and grandness. The upstairs neighbor planted it some twenty years ago when he used to occupy our flat. At about the same time, he also planted the cherry tree near it. The cherry tree is a bit taller than the forsythia and goes unnoticed during the first few weeks of the forsythia's blossoms. Its pink blossoms come later, when the forsythia is just starting to fade, the one replacing the other after a brief period of coexistence.

Between the forsythia and the cherry trees is part of a pear tree that intrudes from across the fence. And on the far side of the cherry tree is a Bramley apple, also with roots in the neighbor's yard. The fullness of its top is in mine. A property line has no meaning for growing plants.

So, various shades of yellow, white, and pink line up before and behind each other. Sometimes, their positions are cleanly marked off, but more often, the colors run together without stops or starts. There are places where the pear stands alone or a long way in front of the next nearest patch of color. Other plants also get to sing an occasional aria – roses, a couple of peonies, a rhododendron. These are about the only indications that the view from the bedroom window is made up of discrete entities.

The yard on the left, where the pear and apple trees have their roots, has long been neglected. The ground floor flat was boarded up some time ago. The nails are rusted, and brown stains run down the rotting plywood. No one has been in the garden for a long time. A shed lies in a fallen heap near one side. It will soon be covered by the steady, aimless growth that covers the surrounding area. I wonder, sometimes, how long it would take for nature to reclaim all of London, if humans disappeared from it. Maybe not long.

The garden to the right of mine is the glorious result of fine growing conditions and the application of much expert human energy. My aged neighbor appears regularly among the daffodils, hair combed just so and wearing a gray cardigan and tie, checking for weeds and making sure all borders are proper. His wife died a few months ago, but he is said to be making a good recovery. I suppose that is in part because she is still out there with him on these fine April mornings. I can see her myself at times.

The birds that have just arrived are starlings, I think. They have taken up residence in the profusion of the abandoned yard on one side, but they fly out of there energetically, swoop across my garden, and plunge into the old man's bird bath. They are so keen on the pleasures of the new season that I speculate further about the woman's death and the man's survival. I fall back on clichés: "life goes on," "the more things change, the more they stay the same," and other East Texas wisdom. I see little out my window but continuation.

A big cat walks the top of the fence, body aquiver at the sight of the birds. Back and forth he paces. My upstairs neighbor saw him a few

IN PASSING. SCENES FROM AN UNCONVENTIONAL LIFE

days ago high in the pear tree far out on a swaying limb, eye to eye with a teasing bird.

It is perplexing to be now in a place where I have longed to be, to have escaped the constraints of small-town life defined by rice fields and oil refineries, but yet not to have left. Many of the places I have been, much of what I have done are out there by the milk on my London doorstep. Where did the idea come from that life is made up of discrete events anyway? My life is not like that. I doubt it's that way for anyone who has given himself fully to the force of a fine spring day.

Hockney, the Brontes, and the Yorkshire Dales
1993

On a recent Friday morning, we drove to a small town in Yorkshire near where David Hockney grew up to see an exhibit of his paintings and to pursue the ghosts of the Brontes who were also from the area.

The show was in a former mohair and woolen mill constructed in the mid-nineteenth century by one Sir Titus Salt. The town – Saltaire – which the mill dominates, is now a gentrified version of a Victorian company town. Parked outside what used to be a grim factory were twin candy-apple red Ferraris. The mill is now scrubbed, well lit, centrally heated, and wired for sound. It functions as an arts mall and office space for telecommuters.

The gallery where Hockney's happy expressions were hung was a single rectangular room perhaps 150 feet by 40, with twenty-foot ceilings. Large windows filled it with light. The warm brightness of the space sent packing the sweatshop misery of the building's first incarnation, and on the afternoon of our visit, we saw the colorful renderings of Hockney élan in what seemed to be a perfect setting. In that place, his merry photo montages and pictures of southern California swimming pools sort of suggested the Victorian notion of progress. The bright liveliness and gaiety of Hockney's work was perhaps a natural defensive response to the cold, dark bleakness of Yorkshire. I figure he took a look around him, and as soon as he could, caught a plane for lotus land and settled there.

After an hour or two with Hockney, we went upstairs to another large room of the old mill and had a salade Nicoise and fizzy water in the company of other tourists before going for a late-afternoon visit to the Bronte parsonage in nearby Haworth. At this time of year, dusk arrives at around 3:30 up there, so it was almost dark as we walked up the steps of the old stone house. It's on high ground with a cemetery sloping off to one side and a somber church down below. The church is a Victorian replacement for the one the Brontes knew.

In the setting, it seemed that the Brontes' creativity was not miraculous in quite the same way as we had thought. To have lived there in the way they lived – quasi sequestered and chilly and entirely lacking central heating, antibiotics, modern plumbing, and the BBC – some form of strong imaginary life would seem to have been the only alternative to madness. Standing on the Brontes' porch shivering in the dark at 4:30 in the afternoon in a town that felt like a part of Appalachia where the mines have closed, it was easy to believe that they simply had to invent other worlds to live in. Anyone would. But, of course, few have invented other worlds so artfully and thoroughly as the Brontes did.

I suspect these ladies would have preferred to go to L.A. with Hockney. It's an interesting picture that – Charlotte and Anne and Emily tanned and healthy, having a glass of chilled Chablis in a fern bar with Dave after a little volleyball on the beach. "Well, like the whole Heathcliff thing was like, you know..." said Emily.

After we had our fill of Bronte-ana, we drove about fifty miles farther north to the Wharfedale area in quest of Highmeadow Cottage, which we had rented for the weekend. The adventure of looking for a particular house in rural England in the dark was one we had experienced before, but we still hadn't gotten the hang of it. In rural areas of England, American-type street addresses do not exist, and one forgets how exotic British English is until it is important to know what a Brit actually means.

We were instructed to go down a certain narrow lane until "on the left you will see a bungalow, and immediately after this you will see the entrance to Highmeadow." Straightforward as those instructions are, they are deceptive and inadequate. The first problem is that in the dark, you will not see "a bungalow." It's almost invisible even in daylight. Truth to tell, it would not have made a lot of difference if it had been visible, since neither of us had any idea at all what the locals meant by "bungalow." The houses in Wharfedale looked pretty much alike to us. Maybe they were bungalows, maybe not. We drove up and down between vaulting hedgerows for an hour or so without success, along the way turning off on a couple of high-center dirt tracks right up to the point where they became impassable.

When at last we encountered someone we could ask for directions, we learned that the critical part of the instructions was the word "bungalow." "Those are not very usual around here," the man said, looking bemused. But he thought there was one back down the road a way. Since I had used the word bungalow for upwards of fifty years, I was not about to admit that I didn't know what one was. So, we just stumbled on and continued to be unsuccessful.

We had rented "cottages" before and were surprised at what the locals meant by that term. Rose Cottage in the Lake District was a three-bedroomed (that's how they put it) unit in a barn that had been converted to a triplex. All I was able to find about "bungalows" after our adventure in the moors and dales was over, was some suggestive but not very helpful remarks about the type of housing enjoyed by civil servants in the raj. Also, bungalows were bigger than cottages. Never mind that Highmeadow Cottage was a bungalow. Nevertheless, the people of Yorkshire distinguish these terms, even though lexicographers have not yet recorded their arcane wisdom. As we drove around, I was reminded of the "mansions" that are all over London, where the term refers to old flats with high ceilings, many of which are down at the heels. The *Oxford English Dictionary* entry for "mansion" indicates that in American usage (lexicographical nose wrinkling here) the word means some sort of large and pretentious dwelling. Imagine that.

We finally pulled over at a phone booth ("call box" in local parlance) and phoned the owner of Highmeadow Cottage. He asked me what I took to be a right silly question. "Are you near an old castle?" I felt certain that we were, since, so far as I knew, we were still in England.

It turned out that "immediate" was a problem, too. The turn we sought came "immediately" after the bungalow only in the sense that there was no intervening turn. In fact, it was way down the road from the Cottage that was a bungalow, which we could not see. We ignorant Yanks thought that immediate meant "coming up pretty dang quick; watch for it."

Eventually, we came upon the owner out on the road waving a flashlight, and he showed us to the cottage. Tea and treacle biscuits had been set out, and a coal fire glowed on the hearth. He told us which window to look out in the morning to see deer, instructed us where to join the public footpaths in the area, and bade us good night. We settled in and had a supper of well-seasoned pinto beans, tortillas, and chipotle salsa, which Ann had made in London. The owner is probably still trying to get that funny smell out of Highmeadow Cottage.

The weather next morning was cloudy and damp, and the temperature was near freezing. We put on woolies, stuffed impermeables into a day pack, and set off rambling, as Brits put it, along the beautiful Wharfe River and up through a moor to a peak called Simon's Seat. An hour or two into the ramble we came to a tea shop where a smiling local greeted us with "Loovely weather, isn't it" in a strong Yorkshire accent. We thought we might have met the designated wiseacre, the one they put out to tease tourists, but she meant it. As it turned out, the weather at that moment *was* "loovely" compared to what followed. When we stopped in again on the way back to the cottage, it was raining. By next morning it was snowing and continued to do so off and on through Monday. We were told that the best time to visit the moors and dales is when the heather and the bluebells are in bloom in the spring, but as it was off season we had the place pretty much to ourselves, and the snow was beautiful.

We rambled and rambled and enjoyed a number of picturesque scenes: pheasants so brightly colored they gave a Hockney touch to an otherwise Currier and Ives display; grouse grousing energetically; a Jack Russell terrier disappearing down rabbit holes and throwing out dirt ferociously; tea and Eccles cakes, tea and treacle sponge with custard, and tea and scones; the artful dance of sheepdogs moving stock down from the high ground in densely falling snow; the ruins of a twelfth century priory, the nave of which survived the dissolution and has since been rebuilt, and still functions as the parish church of St. Mary and St. Cuthbert.

On Monday, I drove Ann to a picture-postcard railroad station in a nearby town to catch an early train back to London. I could see plainly the boys going off to war from that platform, their sweethearts crying and waving hankies, strains of "We'll Meet Again" in the background.

I went back to the cottage, turned in the key, made a stop at a candy shop for local toffee and a tin of Uncle Joe's Mint Balls and, at noon, emerged from this quieter, more innocent England onto the motorway and the trip back to the megalopolis where we live.

Remembering War
1994

While hiking in a remote area of the Lake District on an unusually bright, clear day in autumn, Ann and I came upon a small church high on a hill. As we caught our breath, we read the names on the memorial in the close. It's common for English churches to have such markers to honor the men and women who died in the World Wars. Sometimes, older wars are included as well, and the Falklands conflict, too.

St. John's in the Vale is small. It looks to have seating for about fifty. The parking lot has but two spaces. Yet the stone marker in the yard bears the names of a dozen young men who died in the Great War, the one that was to end all wars. As we stood in the sunshine and read the sad list, we realized that it must have comprised virtually all the boys in every confirmation class for a period of several years. Scarcely a generation later, this quiet little community and many more like it repeated the experience. The names of the young dead from that war are on the opposite side of the marker.

In addition to erecting plaques and monuments, the British honor their war dead each year on Remembrance Sunday with a church service and a secular ceremony. Two things are noteworthy about the observance. The British are officially Christians and their actions on this national holiday reflect the Christian paradox of joy amid sorrow, life in death. And they are as accomplished at public ceremony as they are at fending off aggressors.

* * * *

We take the Underground to Charing Cross Station and walk the remaining few blocks to Westminster Abbey for the national memorial service. For 9:30 on a Sunday morning, a surprisingly large number of passengers are on the train. Many of them wear military service ribbons, medals, and caps. At every stop more get on, until by the time we reach Charing Cross, we seem to be on a crowded troop train, except that the soldiers are old men and women with pot bellies and dowager humps.

On the grounds of the Abbey, flower beds are labeled according to various military units: Royal Engineers, the Cheshire Brigade (who lately served bravely in Bosnia), the Ulster Regiment, Queen's Fusiliers, the Veterinary Corps (whose plot bears a special plea to remember the horses and dogs who made the supreme sacrifice). Names from all around what had been the British Empire are spread across the churchyard: Gurkhas, Bengalese, Jamaicans, Australians, Canadians, and New Zealanders. Poles, Czechs, and Allied Forces are recalled also. One bed is for troops from the United States.

Under a pewter sky, survivors and descendants write the names of dead relatives and fallen comrades on small white crosses and stick them into the soft earth where flowers had been removed for the occasion but soon would bloom again. By the time the service begins, each plot is full to overflowing.

Inside the church sit small groups of active military personnel. There are sailors in the blouses that sailors seem always to have worn and nurses in light blue dresses with dark blue woolen capes. We find seats behind a contingent of Royal Grenadiers, some sort of elite corps made up of men, some so muscular they have to sit turned sideways in order to fit into the seats that were designed for people of ordinary strength and bulk. One young soldier seems unaware that the seam on the back of his coat has a long split. Perhaps he did know, but the solemnity of the occasion dictated that he ignore it for the moment.

The experience is as perplexing as it is exalted.

The wondrous gothic building, raised up over hundreds of years in testimony to man's belief in a God of love, is full of young people trained in warcraft. We speculate that any one of the Grenadiers on the row in front of us can kill almost anyone he wants in a matter of seconds no weapons required. They exude potency and the ability to function in the most trying of circumstances, but they are so young and inexperienced in life's difficulties that one wonders. They pray for those fallen in battle, but most are probably unacquainted with loss. It has not yet occurred to them in any serious way that they too will one day die. And though in church for a solemn religious observation, many have not made the acquaintance of the opening hymn, "O God, Our Help in Ages Past," a very handy hymn, one would think, for soldiers.

Ambiguity is apparent in various other ways as well. The clear impression is that despite having suffered war intensely, the British look back on it with a degree of wistfulness. In the Abbey, there is some sense of the college football victory chant "We're number one" to go along with sadness that things had to be as they were. The ceremony is as much celebration as mourning. It's civic religion at its best and worst.

At a few minutes before 11:00, a procession makes its measured way from a point near the altar through the long nave to the rear of the church where the remains of an unknown soldier rest. The Beadle leads various personages: vicars, choristers, taperers, and the Lord Mayor of Westminster. In final position, splendidly caparisoned official representatives of the five military branches march in solemn dignity, their steps resounding in the silent hall. When the procession is completed, the choir beseeches God that the departed may rest in peace and intones a reminder that "All we go down to the dust; and weeping o'er the grave, we make our song: alleluya, alleluya, alleluya." As the echo wanes, an artillery piece is fired nearby. Those in the church and those gathered with the Queen and Prime Minister to lay a wreath at the Cenotaph keep two minutes of silence. (Old people recall that in years past when the Armistice that ended World War I was still fresh in national awareness, the entire country would go silent.) Afterward, the anti-war prayer of St. Francis is offered up. "Lord, make us instruments of thy peace."

Upon leaving the Abbey, we discover where the grizzled regiments on the Underground troop train had been going. There is, not surprisingly, a parade. Considering the British fondness for pomp and pageantry, this parade is unusually lean and simple. Occasionally, there is a military band in bearskin hats, but it's mostly just old soldiers marching more or less in step taking the applause of a grateful nation.

Some need canes, but even so, manage pretty well to keep the cadence. They stream past St. James Park for a long time, and the cheering never lessens, though occasionally it grows even more enthusiastic, as when units of WRENs pass. The old girls wear the same service ribbons and walk just as tall as the men.

One group of about twenty men who have marched their last buzz past in motorized wheelchairs, sitting as best they can at attention, turn their heads, and salute Prince Charles who is on a curbside reviewing stand. A group of blind men march arm in arm chests out glad to have been of service.

Some come singing softly, exultantly "It's a Long Way to Tipperary" and "Pack Up Your Troubles in Your Old Kit Bag." Without doubt, if their country needs them, they will enlist again and take their gray hair and paunches and their bodies with missing parts right back to the horrors they had but barely survived a long time ago.

Through it all, the British behave like the British. They smile and they laugh and they strut and they march and they pray and they remember and they feel pain and joy at the same time, but through it all, they keep a stiff upper lip. Ann and I weep.

New York City

Lapsed Texan
2003

A lapsed Texan is someone who was reared in the Lone Star faith but who somewhere along the way – more or less willfully and with lamentable inconsistency – has left the fold. I am one. So is Ann.

Thomas Wolfe had it backward for us lapsed Texans. The problem is not that we can't go home again, it's that we can't leave the damned place – not unconditionally. No matter how hard we try, its pulling power is just too strong. Growing up there is like being reared a Roman Catholic; we are enfolded into the secular equivalent of the one true faith and so marked and signed forever and ever.

The furthest we can ever move from that is to lapsed status, and that's not very far, since lapsed Texans, like lapsed Catholics, remain strongly affected by their origins. Of course, we do.

We are told throughout our growing up years that we Texans have a history that is more illustrative of the indomitable human will, courage, resourcefulness, vision, love of democracy, and the basic values of western civilization than that of any people on earth. Of all the states, only Texas has been an independent nation, only Texas has the Alamo, only Texas has defeated a foreign nation in war. Only Texas entertains the belief (highly questionable, though it is) that it has the legal authority to divide itself into five separate states should the desire prove irresistible. And the place is huge – bigger even than Alaska, if you don't count the part of Alaska that is frozen and uninhabitable. Every twelve-year-old knows that Texas has the best pecans, the sweetest grapefruits, the biggest watermelons. Fields of bluebonnets are the stuff of Texas alone. When we were young, only Texas had so much oil. It is God's country; we are God's people.

Then some of us get on a bus to Boston or Dubuque or someplace else not Texas, and almost as soon as we get off, people laugh at us. "Do you really talk that way?" they ask. They let us know that because we grew up where we did (the place we are dead certain God favored above all others) and because we talk funny, we are dumb as dirt, culturally deprived, probably still believe in slavery, and subject to sudden attacks of head lice and hookworms.

Being laughed at gets your attention. Especially if you're me.

I have a Ph.D. and a law degree, I've studied nine foreign languages, enjoyed dinner in hall at Cambridge University, been to Mass at St. Nicholas Cathedral in St. Petersburg, Russia, danced in the streets of Vienna at New Years, walked the Great Wall of China, and taught at the University of Baghdad. One time I went to a party where the guests were so cultivated that two of them got into a heated argument over whether the correct spelling is "Vergil" or "Virgil." Another time I read three paragraphs of Kierkegaard in a single sitting. I find my way to Lincoln Center and Carnegie Hall now and again, mix fancy cocktails on occasion, and rarely pick my nose in public. Never mind all that. As soon as I exchanged a few words with Vinnie, a Brooklyn garbage collector, he called me Bubba.

A simple defensive response is complicated by the realization that we lapsed Texans ourselves carry around a big load of negative feeling about the place. I, for example, hate Texas' narrow-minded parochialism, its nouveau riche vulgarity, its willingness to embrace "dog eat dog" and "an eye for an eye" as civic credos, and its enshrinement of the cowboy as a cultural icon.

Unfortunately for my peace of mind, there is also much about Texas that I hold dear. Wade fishing at dawn off the shore of Mud Island in Aransas Bay is as peaceful an experience as I have ever known. There are buildings in the great cities that are bona fide architectural wonders. It is home to world-class educational institutions, art museums, and medical centers. I like being from this beautiful place,

IN PASSING. SCENES FROM AN UNCONVENTIONAL LIFE

this culture that is so strong, that cuts so bold a figure on the world's stage that the world has to make fun of us. And when I visit Texas, I understand deep in my bones what is around me and who I am.

I've moved away and back many times, but try as I might, I have never been able to move so far away that I leave Texas completely. My vision, my responses, and the way others view me are ordered and shaped by my inescapable Texan-ness. Nevertheless, on the whole, I'm lapsed.

W, Recovering Divider
2002

Some years ago, as Ann was riding her bicycle in Austin, she had an altercation with a man in a car. I don't know exactly what happened or what she said, but I can imagine. Ann has never required assertiveness training. Anyway, after some jawing back and forth, she maneuvered away from the car and rode across the Congress Avenue Bridge and up toward the State Capitol. She must have been especially forthright that day because the man drove after her. When he caught up with her, he ran his window down and fired his biggest verbal gun. "You, you..." he sputtered. "You Yankee lesbian."

Not that it matters especially, but for the record, Ann was born and reared in Texas. Furthermore, if she's a lesbian, it's a part-time calling, and she does just the right thing to keep me from suspecting. But never mind all that.

The man's words revealed more about him than they did about her. To be a woman and a Yankee and a lesbian all rolled into one bicycle-riding package was just the most God-awful thing that Texas man could think of. And based on my many years of living in Texas, I'm sure his way of looking at things was not especially unusual.

Ann and I together once initiated a rather free exchange of views with some fellow Texans about who was going to get pushed off a crowded trail that was shared by walkers, runners, and bike riders. Three sentences into our little colloquy, the guy snarled at us, "Hey, where y'all from, New York?" This, even though Ann and I both talk as country as he did. I guess there was something in the tone of how we told his bunch they were blocking our way.

There used to be bumper stickers on cars all around Austin that read, "If you (heart) New York, go home."

When Ann and I jumped at an opportunity to move to New York City, some people in Texas viewed our action as a betrayal. What in the *hail* had come over us anyway?

Until September 11, the Texan who is President of the whole United States displayed this same antipathy toward New Yorkers. But – not to take this too personally – it wasn't just New York City that he didn't like, it was most cities. He spent August at his ranch near the tiny crossroads settlement of Crawford, Texas. His trip there was characterized as something like going back to the heartland. Over and over, we were told more or less that the President was out where the real people live. I got the impression that in his view, virtue and decency reside exclusively in the hinterland; the coasts and cities are corrupt and sinful. But on September 11, all that changed. He embraced New York City swiftly and completely. Before the attack, it would have been unimaginable.

As a lapsed Texan and a naturalized New Yorker, I'm glad the President has taken this new tack. I'm keeping a wary eye out for backsliding, though. I think of him as a recovering divider, if that.

Upper West Side
1996

When we were planning our move back from London, we decided, if we could afford it, to live on the Upper West Side of Manhattan. We'd had a different New York experience when we lived here before: two versions of Brooklyn – a transitional neighborhood (where Ann got mugged one sunny Saturday at midday on our stoop) and a yuppie ghetto full of precious children and lovely brownstones. Brooklyn was interesting, but it was time for another New York.

We went through the usual process of looking and gagging at rents and raising the maximum amount we were willing to pay and still not finding what we were looking for, until finally we reached a happy outcome.

I started by calling about an ad, and a nice real estate lady newly arrived from Kazakhstan showed me a hovelette that was dangerous, dirty, but relatively inexpensive – $2000 a month plus her standard fee of 15% of a year's rent. After seeing several more that were unacceptable, I asked to see something a little nicer.

In late afternoon on a November day, she took me to see one at Riverside Drive and 104th Street. I stepped off the elevator into a nondescript hallway in the company of a ceremonial escort. To my right was the Kazakh real estate agent. To my left, an off-duty doorman, a short, happy Hispanic who sounded like Jose Jimenez. They must have been elves or something, because on the eleventh floor, a magical thing happened.

The entry was on the east side of the apartment and the windows mostly looked west out over the Hudson River. The setting sun bounced pink and orange off the hardwood floors and white walls transforming an otherwise ordinary 1150-square-foot cube into something to gladden the heart. And the way the place opened out into the western sky and the river below made stepping in as much exit as entrance. The often-crowded confinement of the city ceased to be. For a moment, I was with the children in *The Lion, the Witch, and the Wardrobe* when they slipped through the wardrobe into another world. To be able to look all the way to the horizon and still be in Manhattan was arresting.

After moving in, we soon discovered that besides the sense of opening, the view of the Hudson provided an ever-changing show. Look away for a moment, and when you turn back, it's a different river.

In this winter of dramatic storms, river world has been especially interesting. Last week, we had strong wind – gusts up to 50 mph – and the river was not merely white-capping, it had waves suggesting the open sea. During the coldest periods, I checked often to see if the ice forming along our shore was going to join up with that forming on the New Jersey side several hundred yards away. People say that cars used to drive out to the Statue of Liberty on the frozen river. That's hard to believe, though. It takes a lot to freeze this river. It's brackish, it has a strong current, and it's tidal. The tide and current are apparent in the movement of the ice floes when it's partially frozen. Some of the ice moves downstream on the current. Some of it goes upstream on the tide. I never did see it freeze all the way across.

Barges and small tankers and brightly painted tugboats work their way up and down in designated channels. I enjoyed the better part of one windy afternoon watching a tugboat try to control a large, shiny red vessel. I first spotted them over by the Jersey shore – perilously close to it, I thought. Then the tug moved the big boat into midstream, and the crew dropped an anchor from its bow. It swung around on the anchor in the direction of our bank. If you stand back from the windows, you don't see Riverside Park, which lies between our building and the river, or anything else on land. You see only water and the far

IN PASSING. SCENES FROM AN UNCONVENTIONAL LIFE

shore. It's like being on the deck of a ship. So, when the wind-buffeted vessel started my way, it seemed to be coming stern first into the bedroom. I warned Peewee to be ready to man the lifeboats. The battle of boat against elements was ongoing when I turned to other things. At bedtime, it was still there bobbing and tugging on its tether. I could see shadowy figures moving about on the deck. I hoped they were dressed warmly, because the wind was howling, and it was snowing.

During the night, normal street sounds diminished almost to nothing, and the unnatural quiet woke me. It's a welcome effect of a city snowstorm. And as the snow began to fall more heavily, the light changed to match the quiet. Normally, Manhattan is brightly lit, but heavily falling snow acts like a dimmer switch, softening the look of everything. As the force of the storm built, objects below faded from view. Even lightly falling snow will erase New Jersey, but heavy snow will also take out the treetops and then the ornamental lamps in the park. For most of the night, the view I had been transported by during the day was lost in noiseless, dimly lit snowflakes. I pulled the covers up and gave in to its spell.

Next morning, as I drank coffee and read the paper, it cleared a little, and I was glad to see that my boat was still afloat. After a bit, the tug got its power up, and the two of them moved upstream toward the George Washington Bridge.

Home Again – in Brooklyn
1998

We are enjoying being back in New York after living in Hong Kong. It's the best time of year to be here, and that makes it even more enjoyable. There's a nip in the air, a north wind is bringing in blue sky, leaves are falling, there are apples and pumpkins and greens in the farmers' markets. The Yankees were so good in recent weeks it was possible at times to overlook that they are owned by that jackass George Steinbrenner.

We've found an apartment in the Park Slope neighborhood of Brooklyn. We lived here before, and though gentrification spread and intensified during the years we were away, real estate prices are still somewhat better than in other neighborhoods where we'd like to live. This one is mostly brownstone rowhouses, though there is some limestone construction here and there. Our block, like many, is lined with elms, maples, and what I think are tamarinds. Just now they are very colorful, and each day as the sun moves across, their hues change minute by minute. We have shutters in the windows of the front room. With the bottom half closed, the upper rectangle of the middle window frames a red brick rowhouse across the street, and it looks like someone has hung an Edward Hopper painting behind a screen of yellow leaves.

The ethnic variety of life around here jumps out at us. Our landlord, a painter with a studio in the basement, is an Israeli. He has a young assistant who is a Romanian Christian. His friend, a Greek, is renovating an apartment upstairs. Mohammed does the electrical work. A Chinese family lives next door. Koreans run a little grocery/deli on the corner. Across the street from the Koreans is a shoe repair shop operated by Russians. They know very little English, but their limited facility is sufficient to allow them to laugh at my Texas speech. Across the street from us is a Seventh Day Adventist Church attended mostly, it seems, by African Americans. Enthusiastic hymn singing accompanied by a skating-rink Wurlitzer and drums spills out into the street on Saturday mornings. I took the VCR to a repair shop and found not a single English speaker among the four technicians and three customers. I never did figure out where they were from. Walking home, I passed a Polish Catholic Church. I could go on, but I won't.

The neighborhood has other charms besides ethnic diversity.

There is a fine microbrewery and pub three blocks away.

Prospect Park is especially beautiful right now, and we go there most mornings and jog up and down its hills and past a colonial-period Quaker cemetery and through a Revolutionary War battlefield and by the spot where in 1991, I got into a schoolyard fistfight. My antagonist is still there. We spotted him immediately the first time we went for a run after being away six years. I guess if I were a mensch, I would have taken him on again, but I didn't have the urge. The hospital where I spent a week meditating on my mortality is between us and the park.

A pet-food store down the way has a resident cat who weighs thirty pounds. His name is Fluffy. We watched him sitting on a busy corner one day as a little lap dog on a leash passed by. The dog stayed as far away from Fluffy as his leash permitted and avoided eye contact as if he was on the subway.

A more American and interesting neighborhood would be hard to find.

The Great Saunter
1999

Last Saturday, I took part in The Great Saunter, an annual hike around the thirty-two-mile perimeter of Manhattan Island. It's put on by the Shorewalkers, a group whose mission is to take long walks at the edge of a body of water.

I had envisioned the Saunter as something like the livery of seisin, a feudal ceremony in which a vassal would obtain a freehold interest in a part of a lord's land. In the presence of witnesses, lord and vassal would walk or ride around the plot in question and agree to boundaries. Then the vassal would make symbolic payment by handing the lord a clod of dirt or a clump of grass. He would swear homage and fealty, and so long as he honored his oath to the lord's satisfaction, he got to pretend that he owned the land. In fact, ownership as we understand the term remained with the lord. Still, the vassal came away with a *sense* of ownership and, presumably, an improved attitude.

I had something like the livery of seisin in mind for the Great Saunter. It was time to formalize my appropriation of life as a New Yorker. What better way than to walk the shoreline of Manhattan on a fine spring day while thinking these thoughts? There would be plenty of witnesses, and I could swear fealty, loyalty, or something else to myself or aloud as seemed appropriate at the time. I would have to select someone to play the role of lord, but that would be easy enough.

So, at 7:30 on a sunny morning, I joined about a hundred other saunterers at the South Street Seaport in lower Manhattan. After half an hour of announcements, waiver signing, cap sales, and I don't know what all, we started off in a clockwise fashion around the island. The first encounter with "this isn't quite what I had in mind" came after a few hundred steps when we passed by the wholesale fish market. It was closed for the day, but the smell remained. Immediately following was the detritus of an encampment of homeless people. Then locked restrooms. Then – never mind.

Most people don't know this, but I am an authority on sauntering. My natural gait is something between a saunter and a mosey. When I saw the line of Shorewalkers stretched out a half-mile or so in front of me, I made an expert judgement. "These people are not sauntering. They are stepping out smartly." No problem, though. We would take rest breaks and regroup whenever we came upon a bunch of buses or garbage trucks parked with their diesel engines rumbling. We'd snuggle up close to the tail pipes, breathe deeply, and relax for a while. The Shorewalkers are *tres* New York.

In the beginning, I was not especially bothered about any of this. The view across the harbor to Governors Island, the Statue of Liberty, and Ellis Island was moving, as always. It gave a sense of patriotic pride and gratitude to be a part of this great, unruly city, no matter what eccentric exercise I and a bunch of other people had embarked upon.

We soon rounded the southern tip of the island and started up the west side through Battery Park City. The next 5.9 miles are being developed as a park. At present, it consists mostly of narrow lanes between concrete barriers. Somewhere in that stretch, we stopped for a press conference at which the Parks Commissioner and the governor's man in charge of the fledgling park spoke inaudibly in competition with traffic sounds. I thought one of them might be the right person to hand my lump of dirt to when the time came. Not a good idea, though, as they didn't walk but about a mile.

Everyone agrees that the West Side was less distasteful than most of The Great Saunter. I didn't know that at the time, or I might have just bagged the sauntering and gone to play boccie ball or something else New York.

IN PASSING. SCENES FROM AN UNCONVENTIONAL LIFE

Some of the west side was actually quite enjoyable. The view of the George Washington Bridge and the Hudson stretching beyond it between steep hills and cliffs is a wonder. Also, it was fun to pull back a chain-link fence and walk defiantly through a long section of land being developed by Donald Trump. His minions watched us gimlet-eyed and hostile, walkie-talkies at the ready. I was not afraid, though. I crawled through the fence right behind Ruth Messinger, the Manhattan Borough President. I'd like to see the Donald take on our Ruth. Maybe, I thought, I would give my lump of dirt to her.

Before long, minor frustrations began to add up. No marching songs. No guide pointing out interesting things along the way. For a long time, no lunch. No one had said anything about bringing one either. And no one had warned that the route had been specially designed to avoid all possible encounters with the island's seemingly omnipresent bodegas and not-very-super supermarkets. How is it possible, I wondered, to become dehydrated in the densely populated capital city of the whole world? It was all the more imponderable when at the same time, I was desperate to find a toilet. (I had not yet adopted the New York rule that wherever there is a wall, that is a toilet.) At 2:00, we stopped at a hotdog stand in Inwood Park at the extreme north end of the island. I had two dogs, an ice cream bar, some M&Ms, and two cokes and felt better.

We were told that the next segment, which ran southeast along the Harlem River, would be a little harder. I asked several people – who, inexplicably, were doing this trek a second or third time – what "harder" meant. No one knew. It was, though.

The next three hours were not exactly shorewalking. We saw a lot of Harlem River Drive (a highway) and Harlem streets jammed with boom cars blasting salsa or rap (no Bach), but not much of the Harlem River. That was disappointing. I had hoped to see a floater or two.

Along about the fifteen-mile point, a bunch of the less committed got on the subway. Those of us who were left kept getting broken up into increasingly smaller groups. I began to sense that things were starting to come apart seriously when conversation became a repetition of "I think that's them up there." Occasionally, a local would offer, "your friends turned right at the next corner." I can't imagine how they spotted us so easily. It wasn't like we were wearing uniforms or anything.

At St. Nicholas Avenue and 185th Street, the Shorewalkers' president said he was going to wait for some stragglers. He and they would go around another way and meet the rest of us a mile or so farther on. Sure he was. He was dropping out. I said adios and jogged up a long, long hill to catch a group of about ten who were taking what seemed to me the proper route. When I caught up to them, I saw that what they were taking was the subway.

I saw some Shorewalkers about a half mile farther on alongside a sort of highway. I jogged a while and caught up with them. It wasn't long until I realized they had no idea at all how to get anywhere close to the Harlem River and a shore. But since we had run out of subways, and there were certainly no taxis cruising the area, there was nothing for it but to keep on walking.

We asked directions here and there and did the best we could. This was at about the sixteen-to eighteen-mile point, I think. (The organizational geniuses who've been putting on this event for years had not bothered to mark any distances.) That was far enough along that we had finally slowed to a true saunter, and saunter we did. We sauntered over highway garbage accumulated in a three-foot strip between the highway guardrail and a chain link fence. We sauntered (maybe staggered is more accurate) over thirty-foot high heaps of asphalt pieces, a dump for streets that had been scraped up. We sauntered through a half-acre cache of road salt. We sauntered by homeless encampments. Sauntering was morphing into trudging when the Triborough Bridge and the East River appeared. That was a much-needed pick-me-up.

IN PASSING. SCENES FROM AN UNCONVENTIONAL LIFE

Before long, I was trudging along with but one other person. Occasionally, we spotted one or two of our group ahead or behind. At about twenty-eight or twenty-nine miles, in front of Gracie Mansion, the mayor's official residence, my trudging partner got on a bus.

It was then that I experienced the return of common sense. I became aware of a lot of stuff all at once. I had blue ribbon blisters on both feet, my back was in spasm, I was still several miles from the finish, and no matter how often I scanned the East River esplanade, I couldn't spot a single other person of the hundred or so I'd started out with. It was a Boy Scout snipe hunt, and I was the tenderfoot.

Before abandoning the saunter, I toyed with the idea of knocking on the mayor's door to see if I could hand him a symbol of my payment. No clod of dirt either. I'd give him one of the syringes I'd been stepping on along the way. Maybe he'd think again about closing the methadone clinics. He probably wouldn't have answered the door, though. But no matter. I had decided up in Harlem that the livery of seisin analogy was not the right metaphor. What I'd been doing all day was more like a tomcat spraying here and there marking his territory willy-nilly.

Whatever the analogy, New York is now mine in a way it wasn't before last Saturday.

Bronx Hardware Store
1999

Now that we've moved again, our neighborhood hardware store is on Broadway across from the Meat-o-Mat and under the elevated tracks of the 1/9 subway at a point where the upscale Riverdale neighborhood becomes the real Bronx. I went over one day to do some shopping.

I waited a long time for a skinny young clerk to help me. People were calling him Flaco. Flaco was Hispanic – probably either Puerto Rican or Dominican. Not that it makes any difference which. It's just that recognizing the difference is evidence of a full set of New York tools. I'd like to be so skilled.

Flaco went behind the counter and handed me several sizes of the masonry drill bit except the 1/4-inch one I had come for. After what seemed to be about a half-hour of this, during which Flaco waited on other customers in addition to me, I developed a strong urge to go behind the counter myself where I would be close enough to read the labels. It was not to be, of course. Customers were not permitted within reading distance of anything smaller than a snow blower.

Flaco handed me a 9/16-inch bit, and I said again, "no, 1/4 inch," and then the curtain rose on a rather fully developed little drama featuring an interesting new customer with a serious problem. I call it "The Helpful Hardware Man. A Parody."

I knew something was up as soon as I saw her. She was Anglo – badly bleached blond, chunky, and Anglo. Her problem had to do with a toilet.

"I flush it, and the water goes down, but a lot of the uh, the uh – you know – the stuff – stays up." Looking at her, I would not have thought she'd have the least bit of trouble saying the name of the substance that wouldn't go down when she flushed. That reluctance gave her character a degree of fullness, kept her from being flat.

Flaco, the helpful hardware Puerto Rican/Dominican man, played dumb. Maybe he wasn't playing. He asked, "You mean like cigarettes?" I thought that an odd response, but then I was a stranger in those parts.

"Yeah, and uh, you know..."

"You got to wrap the cigarette butt in a little bit of tissue, you know. It's too light, so it's gonna float." He conducted this tutorial on the fundamentals of the sanitary sewer over his shoulder. His body was still turned toward the display of drill bits.

At that point, I had a sudden realization. The man was multi-tasking. In fact, as I looked around, I saw that every clerk in the place was multi-tasking. According to any number of social commentators – all of whom find it easier to get published than I do – multi-tasking is the province of top-of-the-heap type people, people who are burdened with cell phones and Palm Pilots. Those writers should spend some time in the Bronx.

The lady seemed to think she hadn't been clear. She tried again. "But see nothing goes down but the water."

"You got to use a snake, then," Flaco said.

I had a picture of this worn-looking woman buying a plumber's snake and jamming it deep into the sewer lines of the broken-down apartment building where she lived. She seemed to be looking at the same picture. Her eyes went blank for a moment, then she shuffled out, head down. It was one of those plays that without warning switches from light comedy to spirit-draining pathos.

I shook it off.

"That may be the bit I'm looking for up there on the second row," I said helpfully.

At that moment, the English-only manager came stage center. Peter, he was, barged in with a Spanish-only customer who wanted information about some cabinets that were on sale. Flaco, about whom

IN PASSING. SCENES FROM AN UNCONVENTIONAL LIFE

I had come to feel somewhat possessive, was pressed into service. He took the customer toward the display, and I claimed Peter.

Now, it should be kept in mind that the story of the woman with the toilet problem was a play within a play. The principal play, which provides the frame for the others, is about me and my problems. Would I be able to purchase what I had come for? Would I leave the store still believing that I was a reasonably functional person? More important, would I get finished before the parking meter expired? (The fine is high – I think $55.) Most importantly – this was the real ticking-time-bomb source of suspense – would I get out before I peed in my pants?

That little hardware store under the elevated tracks was a great leveler. Given the experience I was having, I might as well have been poor.

I got aggressive with Peter, the manager, hoping by doing that to get a little respect. I spoke loudly and used the New York question form that seeks to elicit guilt along with information.

"You don't have a 1/4-inch masonry bit?" I said querulously. He could not possibly have missed the elliptical part – "you dumbass."

"A what?" Peter was frowning. I don't think he liked questions. I'm sure he didn't care for this particular one.

"A 1/4-inch masonry bit."

"A what?" He had gone to the loud bray of interrogatory sound that is a New York specialty. If he was not annoyed, he fooled me.

"A drill bit for use on bathroom tile."

"Oh. A masonry bit." He rhymed "masonry" with "missionary." It's no wonder that I have a recurring dream in which the authorities rescind my Ph.D. in applied linguistics. It's obvious I don't deserve to have one or I would already have picked up this variation in pronunciation from talking with Flaco.

Peter was looking for the 1/4-inch size when the helpful Puerto Rican/Dominican hardware man and the Spanish-speaking lady re-entered from stage right. She had questions that were beyond Flaco's ken. Could the installer get to her apartment in time to meet the deadline on the sale price?

Peter adopted a blank look and said, "The cabinets aren't on sale."

"It's on the flyer," Flaco said.

"That price applies only to the cabinet." I flashed back to the time I tried to read Kierkegaard. Then Peter clarified everything.

"The counter that goes on top is regular price."

A topless cabinet being somewhat limited in utility, the lady asked for time to mull it over.

Before she could work it out, a newcomer – yet another Anglo – butted in. He was a middle-aged guy with Irish-tinted speech. His rosy cheeks and the broken capillaries on his nose suggested that he spent a good deal of time in the pubs on the next block.

"Would you have a knife for cutting window board?" he asked.

It was such a passing strange question that I ignored the way he had interrupted the Spanish-speaking woman who had interrupted me. By my count I was either three or four removes from where I needed to be to buy the 1/4-inch drill bit, which was not a good situation since I needed to pee so bad.

Tough. We were off and running on another little play, this one formed primarily around the question – what *is* window board? – and secondarily – "how would you cut such a thing with a knife?" Everyone with ears to hear was sucked into the developing drama.

"Window board?" Peter asked.

"No. Window board."

"Window board?"

"No. Window board."

We strained to focus our little gray cells. Every face bore evidence of the effort. Pity there was no photographer. It struck me as quite likely that it was in this store or one like it that method acting had been born. Had Stanislavsky shopped here? I would ask, if I got another turn to speak.

IN PASSING. SCENES FROM AN UNCONVENTIONAL LIFE

Finally, by some happenstance I don't recall, it became clear that the Irishman was asking about a knife to cut a product named "Wonder Board."

As soon as Peter understood that, he got right on top of things.

"Oh. Wonder Board."

"Yeah. Window Board."

"You need a tungsten blade knife."

"I know that." He knew that? "Do you have any?"

"No. We've got 'em at our other stores, but none here."

The Irish guy exited stage left, no doubt intending to stop in at the first pub he came to and add a bit more color to his cheeks. Maybe he'd run into the lady with the toilet problem. They could drink together and take turns telling each other what a hard day it had been.

* * * *

I made it home without getting a parking ticket or wetting my pants. And finally, by buying a set of six *masonary* bits in various sizes, I had obtained the 1/4-inch size that I had gone through so much for.

I mixed a martini, put some Camembert and crackers on a plate, and collapsed on the living room couch. Peewee made a place on my lap, and we watched the sun go down behind the New Jersey palisades on the other side of the Hudson.

Life in this new neighborhood was going to be hard work.

Moving as Dying
2014

It's said that at the moment of death, your whole life passes before your eyes. I've not yet experienced death, so I don't know about that. I have, however, changed residences repeatedly – to the best of my recollection, forty-one times just since 1960, and every time I've done it, something quite like my whole life has passed before my eyes. Not as discrete events in sequence, though. It was more a clutter of recollections and emotions and half-forgotten urges; sometimes in layers taking turns being on top; sometimes tumbling about like clothes in a dryer.

I once met a middle-aged farmer in northern Wales who had never lived in a house other than the one he was born in. I cannot fathom such a life. I'm sure that moving as often as I have is a little unusual, and that to some extent I have been formed by it. But living in the same house your whole life is beyond unusual. Way beyond. What was the effect of never starting over from time to time? I wish I'd stayed in Wales longer and gotten to know him.

Some of the relocations Ann and I have made were paid for by Ann's law firm. They were generous and all encompassing. The moves to London and Hong Kong included even Peewee's air fare and six months of quarantine at a posh cattery in London. Even taking our car to England was paid for.

A crew of strangers would show up, seal the artifacts of our life in numbered cartons, give us papers to sign, load it all onto a truck, and drive away. At the other end, a different crew of strangers would show up hauling our stuff in a truck. Piece by piece they would lug it into rooms that we had only a few hours' acquaintance with and annoy us repeatedly with a question we were ill-prepared to answer. "Where do you want this?" At some point late in the day, we'd sign more papers and distribute tips, and the crew would drive away leaving us to sift and sort and reflect on where we'd been and where we were going and what it's all about.

Those moves were different from moves we've initiated and paid for ourselves. Brooklyn to the Bronx, for example.

The first company I called asked, "How many boxes of kitchen goods do you have?" Then, "How many boxes of books do you have?" I had no idea, of course, but the man was oh-so understanding. "That's all right, Mr. Willcox. That's all right."

He phoned back after a quarter of an hour with a price – $450. Since we had almost 300 items on the inventory of our recent move back from Hong Kong, I was skeptical. Was that price guaranteed? Well, no, not exactly. It was based on so much per hour and an estimate of how many hours it would take. But I was not to worry. These guys were good. They were Israeli army veterans. Was I to infer that Israeli soldiers get special training in how to pack dishes and reassemble furniture maybe so they can handle relocation to the West Bank of settlers they then had to protect?

I gave the voice on the phone a response that is probably still being talked about in Brooklyn moving and storage circles. I told him I wouldn't do business with him because his price was too low. My answer machine ran red hot over the next several days. The company had reconsidered; how did $1400 sound?

No matter how the transfer of possessions is handled, it involves hours and hours of picking over the detritus of a lifetime – the souvenirs, the long-unworn clothes, and the odd bits that had begun to lose whatever power they'd once had. Finally time to throw it away? Yes? No?

IN PASSING. SCENES FROM AN UNCONVENTIONAL LIFE

T. S. Eliot barges in uninvited. "Time present and time past are both perhaps present in time future, and time future contained in time past".

There is a sixty-three-year-old T-shirt with the words "Beaumont Jr. Softball League" on the front. One look at it, and I'm sweating under the lights of Beaumont's Central Park, trying to keep the infield dirt from making me so muddy that I'd be an even sorrier catcher than I was when clean, and inhaling the DDT sprayed by the mosquito truck as it passed behind the backstop, and hoping that big bastard Robert Hansen didn't run over me at the plate again.

A fraternity pledge manual that I've kept with the still-unrealized intention of having a careful look at it so I can figure out why I ever thought I needed to have that experience. Early Hi-Fi recordings that go by the quaint name LPs. Almost everything I've ever published from "Randall Jarrell's Eschatology" to multiple copies of *A Franklin Manor Christmas*. A yellowing manuscript of an unfinished novel. The daily budget for a high school trip to Europe.

And the photographs. (Nothing makes Eliot's point more emphatically.) You think you'll open just one container that has been waiting for years to be sorted and stored in some orderly fashion and the next thing you know you've spent the afternoon being whipped through all sorts of emotions in a way that leaves you limp and thirsty and looking around for someone to bore with their stories.

Brits use the expression "moving house." Here in the colonies, we just say "moving." I believe our term is more accurate. "Moving house" suggests that the experience is less complex and more mechanical than any I've ever experienced. "Moving" involves far more than transporting goods from point A to point B and going to sleep in a new bedroom. And contrary to reasonable expectation, it is definitively nonlinear.

When the van is at the curb, it's clear that I didn't live in Beaumont then move to Austin then to Washington and so on. Residences accrete; they don't replace each other. I can't look for a new dwelling without having in mind the search for one in Baghdad with an Iraqi real estate agent who bragged that his cousin was an "assistant expert" with the U.N. and being shown flats in London by a happy fellow who crowed that his girlfriend was a "dirty little thing" who would "do anything" and being told by New York landlords that they did not rent to lawyers.

With so many scenes going on simultaneously, it's no wonder moving is exhausting.

Ann and I have just experienced another one. We sold our New York City apartment and made a former sanatorium/monastery in the Adirondacks our only residence.

We put the apartment on the market in January and received an offer about three weeks later. The buyer's financial statement looked good, and we anticipated closing soon, not, as it turned out, in the middle of June.

While waiting, we began to spend more time in Saranac Lake, sort of trying out gradually the feeling of being full-time residents. To save money, we cut off the apartment phone, internet connection, and TV cable. I also abandoned garage parking ($600 + per month) and returned to parking on the street and fighting the inconvenience of street-sweeping regulations. I had engaged in this twice-a-week, move-it-and-find-a-new-spot routine during our less prosperous early years in the city. I thought mistakenly that it would not be difficult to pick up this skill again.

On a Friday morning in early spring, I went out to move the car before the 8:30 start of sweeping. I drove around for about twenty minutes and found a new place. I wheeled skillfully into it, drawing what I thought was admiring attention from passersby. (New Yorkers are ridiculously unskilled at parallel parking.) I locked up with a no-look, over-the-shoulder click of the fob and strutted away feeling real good about being able to park on the street in New York City.

IN PASSING. SCENES FROM AN UNCONVENTIONAL LIFE

I was still feeling good about it two days later as I strolled home from church thinking pleasant thoughts of the nice Sunday lunch and nap that lay just ahead. That was when I discovered nothing but space along the curb where I'd parked. The space I had so cleverly made use of on Friday was in a NO PARKING zone in front of a synagogue. My skills were rustier than I had thought.

I made some phone calls and found my way to the tow pound on Hudson River Pier 76. There, I joined about thirty people waiting for a turn at post-office-thick windows behind which grumpy clerks "measured out their lives with coffee spoons." (Eliot again.)

The fine was $205 plus $20 for storage plus a punitive charge of $5.15 for using a credit card. (Cash was acceptable, but, as a sign indicated, no pennies.)

As the clerk read my insurance papers, registration card, and driver's license, I spotted a notice that said all three must have the same address. Uh oh. Two of mine were in the city, one in Saranac Lake. I feared I had wasted my Sunday afternoon coming down to this grim bastion of traffic regulation and they would keep the Prius and I'd have to go home defeated and it would be like the time when I was working in the City of New York's Division of Code Enforcement and was directed to tell a man who had been selling watermelons without a permit that his confiscated truck would not be returned and he had no right of appeal. (I quit that job.) In a film or book, the actual outcome of my nonmatching-addresses problem would have been implausible; the grumpy clerk just didn't notice.

I handed my release papers to a uniformed attendant, and she drove me and several fellow miscreants to our cars.

A parking ticket, limp and almost illegible from being snowed on, was stuck under the wiper blade – $65 for parking in a prohibited space. After all the paying I'd already done, that seemed like piling on.

The car was filthy, so after liberation I ran it through the car wash that was handily situated near the pound. It was a sort of Macbeth action for cars. In a perfect world, the city would have offered that service free of charge to give offenders a clean start to their driving lives.

While waiting on the sidewalk by the exit, I tried to recover the little bit of equanimity I occasionally enjoy. I hadn't gotten far with it when I inadvertently stuck the receipt for the $21 wash into the locked tip box, thus making it impossible to present it and claim the Prius.

I can manage enough Spanish to get a beer and important things like that, but persuading a car-wash crew to find the one person in the city who had the key to the enormous padlock on the tip box was challenging. The crew took a break and gathered around to be entertained by my efforts. Finally, since my car was blocking the exit ramp, they waved me on. I went directly from the car wash to a parking garage.

New York City garages post rates in large letters the way gas stations do. They shout their appalling tariffs shamelessly. In my neighborhood, it was $12.67 for the first hour. After that, the rate per hour declined. The maximum for twenty-four hours was $33.79. Fine print at the bottom of the signs revealed tax of 18.375%, making the total charges an even $15 for one hour and $40 for twenty-four hours.

I needed about twenty-five hours before Ann and I would drive to Saranac Lake. I didn't like it, but I figured $55 was cheaper than another trip to the tow pound. Before leaving, I checked my arithmetic with the attendant. It was a good move. He and all New York City garages use a form of arithmetic in which $40 + $15 = $80. A careful reading of the rate sign revealed all. "Max to 24 hours – $40. Each add'l 24 hours *or part thereof – $40.*" (Italics mine.)

I asked the guy what would happen if I redeemed the car a minute short of twenty-four hours, paid $40, drove around the block, then put it back in the garage for a single $15 hour.

"You staying over there at the Belnord Hotel?" he asked. I inferred the force of his question to be in regard to a special rate for guests. It

IN PASSING. SCENES FROM AN UNCONVENTIONAL LIFE

wasn't. The look on his face said it all. He just wanted to confirm his suspicion that I was from out of town. He explained wearily.

"Look. Just come in before twenty-four hours are up, I'll close out your ticket, and start you a new one."

"No charge of two times $40?"

"No."

"No need for me to drive around the block?"

"No."

It seemed an odd (though welcome) practice.

Walking to the apartment, I recalled that the tow-pound rate had been only $20 a day. I should have left the Prius there until we were ready to leave town. I can't imagine why the city is charging only half the market rate. Mayor Bloomberg didn't get to be a billionaire doing things like that.

Some years earlier, I got into a conversation with a casual acquaintance, who like many New Yorkers didn't own a car and didn't know how to drive. She had started a driver's ed course once, but after a couple of days of sitting in stalled traffic on West Side Highway practicing various ways of giving the finger to fellow motorists, she gave up on getting a license. I wish she had stayed with it. I would have liked hearing more about how people were trained to drive in the city. Surely the course included a unit on the nuances of parking.

* * * *

Our last day as residents of the city began with quotidian chores – dealing with parking (see above), but also packing the iron, vacuum cleaner, coffee pot, and the futons on which we'd spent our final night, arranging for one final coat of paint on a recently repaired wall, and making the apartment "broom clean" (a condition subject to interpretation) – all before the buyer's pre-closing walk-through at 12:30. Normal people would not have found these small tasks especially demanding, but at this point, Woody Allen replaced T.S.

Eliot. To us, the list threatened negative outcomes that ranged from failure to close the sale to all-encompassing defeat and dishonor by which we would be forever defined. We endured an anxious night in the lead-up and drank our morning coffee in silent admiration of people who manage to deal gracefully with real pressure.

What if the buyer wanted to argue that we had not met the contingencies of his offer? It seemed a strong possibility; to represent him in the transaction he had suspiciously engaged a litigator, not a real estate attorney. If we couldn't get everything into the car, which was surely going to be the case, what would we leave on the sidewalk? Was there a fine for doing that? What if the car got towed again when I parked it on the street for long enough to load our stuff?

It had to be moved by 8:30 for street sweeping, so off I went on another driving adventure. I pulled away from the curb just in time to join a line behind a stop-and-go garbage truck. I did that a second time on a different block while looking for another parking place. In the process, I came to regret that I was a coffee drinker. When not thinking about my bladder, I occupied myself with trying to figure out what there was in Steve Inskeep's delivery that made him sound so condescending.

After a bit, I gave up on finding a parking space on the street and pulled into the garage that I'd quit as too expensive some months earlier. The same grumpy Romanian ex-pat was on duty. Having thoroughly adapted to life in the city, he yelled at me like a native when I stopped in the wrong place. Two hours and five minutes later, he was in a better humor – smiling actually – as he charged me $30 for three hours (cash only).

While the car was threatening financial ruin, Ann and I packed and cleaned and discarded things until the apartment was empty and tidy. We managed to get everything into the car. We said our goodbyes. And then it was time to go.

IN PASSING. SCENES FROM AN UNCONVENTIONAL LIFE

To live in a well-run doorman building is to be taken care of in a most agreeable way. It's assisted living with autonomy intact. Staff members provide protection from intruders, they repair things that break, and (in our case at least) they offer constant good cheer and affection. They and we were sorry to part. But it was time to go.

We fought our way through heavy traffic to a different garage, one that would allow us to park and lock the fully loaded car. (In most garages, an attendant buries the car somewhere deep inside and keeps the keys.) Then in an unexpected and most welcome turn of events, the day's tempo changed from presto to andante.

We picked up take-out food and slowly, deliberately strolled to the elm grove in Central Park, took a seat on a bench, and enjoyed a leisurely picnic. It was a beautiful, sunny day with the temperature in the seventies. Nearby, three men fresh from the Andes played Andean music. When they took a break, we could hear a lone saxophonist farther down the way playing American standards. After lunch, a high school orchestra struck up in a nearby band shell. The quality of the performances was mediocre at best, and normally we would have sought a spot free of mediocre-at-best music. On this occasion, we welcomed it.

It was our last day to live in the city, and it was the first time in our years there that we'd taken time for a picnic in the park. It was a moment far from the New York that had often bedeviled us. As we were remarking that ordinary in-your-face New York would be much easier to leave, a middle-aged man in a long black coat walked past led by a woman holding a chain attached to his three-inch-high rhinestone choker.

We made our way to the closing, signed lots of documents, and in due course emerged onto Lexington Avenue divested of the apartment and our identity as New York City residents. After a $20 taxi ride and a final parking fee ($36), we edged our way into stop-and-go traffic on

PAUL WILLCOTT

West Side Highway and drove three hundred miles north to a new life in a mountain village.

That Feeling-at-Home Feeling
2021

I feel more at home in New York City, especially the Upper West Side of Manhattan, than in any place I have lived as an adult. I've been trying to figure out why this should be. For that matter, why does anyone feel at home anywhere? And what does "feeling at home" even mean?

I've felt totally at home only one other time. During World War II, when my dad was employed in defense work at a refinery in Iran, my brother, mother, and I moved a thousand miles to live with my maternal grandparents in Muskogee, Oklahoma where my parents grew up. Being there felt perfectly right. I have some ideas about why, but to do them justice would require a long book that probably wouldn't interest even my children, so I make do with boring Ann from time to time with recollected experiences and images. What they all point to is that the adults I was surrounded by were utterly happy to be who they were. I can't say how much of that was a result of the place and how much came from within. In any case, we lived in a small house and had little money. But we wanted for nothing, material or otherwise. When my dad returned after eighteen months, economic necessity took us to live in another way in a different place. For one reason or another, I've been on the move ever since. [For a medium length treatment of the time in Muskogee see *12,000 Miles of Road Thoughts. Old Van, Old Man, Recovering Hippie, Dying Cat*, Wordstruck Press, 2023.]

For me, feeling fully at home requires a sense that I'm not out of step, a requirement not well met in most circumstances of my life. As a teenager I didn't like thinking I was the only person in high school who supported Adlai Stevenson for president or feeling discomfort at those windy Bible Belt invocations at football games. And if anyone else in town aspired to a cosmopolitan life of books and music, I never met that person. College days could have been perfect – I was in an elite liberal arts program and studied with gifted teachers – if I'd had enough money so that I wasn't always working when everyone else was studying or dating. Living in Washington D.C. during the Kennedy years was exciting and promising, but I couldn't get satisfying work. And so on.

Feeling at home is not an on-off matter, of course. It's a continuum. I've lived in a couple of places that were way down at the bottom of the comfort scale and others that were up near the top. To make matters more puzzling, in two of the near misses, I was definitively alien – Baghdad in the sixties and London in the nineties.

In New York City, it's common and acceptable to be from somewhere else. Thirty-six percent of its population is foreign born. Cradle New Yorkers are very likely a minority. That means my being born and reared in a refinery town on the Texas coast does not prevent me from being a full New Yorker.

Besides that, there is much in everyday New York life that is to my liking. As a big-government, tax-and-spend liberal, I am among my own people as surely as if we were blood relatives. There are any number of people on this island, some right in my neighborhood, probably in my apartment building, for whom classical music, theater, art museums, and lectures are a great pleasure, even a passion. There are vegan restaurants close by (some offering entrees other than grain bowls and veggie burgers). I'm able to practice my Anglo-Catholic faith. (In many places I've lived, it has been less well known than Zoroastrianism.)

Things such as these do a lot to make me feel at home here, but they aren't the whole story. The fundamental cause is inexplicable and inexpressible. It's about feeling good walking down the street, feeling free to start a conversation with anyone on any subject, being

IN PASSING. SCENES FROM AN UNCONVENTIONAL LIFE

comfortable with who I am (the way my family was in Muskogee), and knowing in some way that it's the right place for me to be.

If I ever figure out how this works, I'll let you know.

My River
2022

Rivers are magically, irresistibly alluring. Huckleberry Finn felt it. So, it seems, did John the Baptist. The Ganges has full-blown religious significance. Akiko Bush swam nine of them and wrote an excellent book about it. (*Nine Ways to Cross a River. Midstream Reflections on Swimming and Getting There from Here.*)

My river is the Hudson, tangible but ineffable.

For Christians, the miles of benches along its Manhattan bank are as church pews. Churches are closed just now, but the river offers a full range of services: hymns, pleas for deliverance, celebration of blessings, communion with saints, and recitation of Psalms. All silently, of course, and that lacks the affirmation that comes from joining with others in profession of faith. Still, quiet time alone beside the river is of inestimable value. To the religious and secular alike it can offer transcendent renewal.

Most mornings, I leave my phone at home, turn off my hearing aids, and walk down to the river to say hello and pay my respects. On busy days, I just nod and acknowledge its presence, like Jim Chee, the Navajo protagonist of the Tony Hillerman novels. Chee begins his days by tossing a pinch of corn pollen into the air in ritual appreciation of his place in the natural order. But increasingly of late, I sit for a few minutes and let the river have its way with me. Many people do. I find their numbers reassuring in this time when the search for distraction seems ever more compelling. Of course, some bench sitters study their smart phones. When I see that happening, I'm tempted to say, "Hey, buddy, you're missing a lot," or more directly, "Repent. You're sinning against the spirit of the river."

Not being burdened by electronic gadgets, dogs are really good at being present. Some sit on benches pressed up against their human companions, gazing at the river, exulting in the almost-autumn sunshine, quite at home on the limen. They seem to be reflecting. Maybe they are.

The Amtrak passes through the park that's between my apartment and the river. So does the West Side Highway. But the train is out of sight, its tracks buried beneath concrete and landscaping by Robert Moses and the parks department during the 1930s. The highway is somehow not as noisy as such busy thoroughfares usually are. Now and then, a motorcycle with modified pipes or the screaming siren of an emergency vehicle obtrudes, but trucks and buses are not permitted on it. Most of the time, a steady hissing hum is all the sound that reaches me on my riverside bench.

The river changes day by day. I suppose a careful and trained observer could see it change moment by moment. The tide is always moving in my part of the Hudson; sometimes it has in it more of the ocean a few miles downstream, sometimes more of the Adirondacks where it starts. On a winter day with a strong northwest wind, it's fierce, white-capping, and frightening. Some days in summer, when the wind takes a rest, it's quiet as a farm pond. A shower last week was so strong it made the river go dark, and New Jersey, a few hundred yards away, became invisible.

Through a speeded-up natural variation of the right of adverse possession, I have taken ownership of the river. It's immaterial that other bench sitters and dogs own it too. It's *my* river.

Adirondacks

A Powerful House
1999

On a luminous autumn day in 1998, Ann and I drove three hundred miles from our apartment in Brooklyn to the Adirondacks village of Saranac Lake to have a look at a monastery that was for sale. We weren't really in the market for a monastery, but it sounded interesting, and it wasn't too expensive, so we went.

Before it became a cloistered home for Carmelite nuns, it was a tuberculosis sanatorium. We expected to find a squared-away, masonry building that looked institutional. We were wrong. It was a decaying, bright-yellow, 12,000-square-foot, Queen Anne Victorian house that goes every which way. It sits on a rise and looks out on a lake, the village, and the mountains beyond.

Two quick walk-throughs and we knew.

As a dwelling, it is large and unique. It has around forty rooms, depending on what is meant by 'room.' There are two active kitchens and a bakery, two more kitchens that are no longer used, an ice-house, a confessional, four fireplaces, a wooden folding-door phone booth, a soundproof phone room with a cutoff to enable privacy (presumably for use by the Prioress when conducting official business), many embossed tin ceilings, wainscoting all over the place, an elegant three-story staircase of quarter-sawn oak, a fairly new-looking basketball goal in the driveway, a laundry room with a machine plus two washboards that bear the words, "Do not rub hard. The board will do the work." Before Vatican II, when the nuns came out of cloister, there was a dentist's office, but nothing is left of it now, blessedly, not even that old-fashioned-dentist's-office smell. There used to be a burial plot, but the nuns who rested there were taken away during the lead-up to closing.

The house has come to be looked on as a sort of civic asset held in common by the people of the village in the way parks and the library are. Locals have been keen, perhaps anxious, to know what plans we have for the house. They are always pleased when we tell them we're going to fix it up in a historically appropriate way and just enjoy it as a vacation retreat rather than turn it into a B&B or something else commercial. We have moments when, despite the mortgage, we feel like we are mere trustees for the real owners, the townspeople. I have a theory about how this sense of community ownership came about.

It was built as a personal residence in the 1890s. Not long after, when open-air treatment of tuberculosis became the primary industry in town, cure porches (unheated sleeping porches) were added to most of the bedrooms, and the house morphed into Franklin Manor, a relatively grand sanatorium, what is called locally a cure cottage. A brochure for it boasted twenty-six bedrooms, but not counting the cure porches, we count about half that many. In 1952, when open-air treatment of tuberculosis had been replaced by drugs, it was given to the church, and Discalced Carmelite nuns moved in. From the beginning, they were a strong force in the life of the predominantly Roman Catholic village. It seems everyone has a story to tell about some personal interaction with the nuns.

The house draws power from being an integral part of the history and culture of the community. And it has gotten inside Ann and me and made us feel its strong force in a personal way.

My life has been characterized in large measure by restlessness. I've tried all manner of ways of being – lived here, lived there, done this, done that – but never managed to find anything that seemed to be really me. Such a history has led me to wonder from time to time if maybe something is wrong with me. Though less afflicted than I, Ann has been restless too, especially in recent years.

IN PASSING. SCENES FROM AN UNCONVENTIONAL LIFE

One autumn day before we had closed on the purchase, I stood on the lawn under a canopy of brilliant yellow sugar maples and told the Prioress my story of restlessness. I really got rolling with it, and at the last I heard myself saying, "It's ironic that after a lifetime of searching and not finding something of special social value that also suited my talents and limitations, here I am at age sixty about to be defined by – of all things – a parcel of real estate." That's a little overstated, I suppose, but still, when I looked up at the old house that in its life had gone several different directions, I was given a moment in which I could take a deep breath and feel for maybe the first time in my life that it's OK to be me. It's a powerful building that can do that.

Though Ann wouldn't put all this in quite the same way, I think she is having about the same experience.

Pell, Bill Gruber, and the Flag
2001

My grandmother's name was Pearl, but we kids called her Pell. Pell was very patriotic. As the Fourth of July approaches, I've been thinking about Pell, a young soldier called Bill Gruber, and the flag.

Pell spent some of her later years in an assisted living center in Muskogee, Oklahoma's Honor Heights Park, a memorial to those who have fought our wars. There was a flagpole on the sloping lawn below her apartment, and her building was near the VA Hospital.

During World War II, when my mother and my brother and I lived with Pell and my grandfather, young soldiers sometimes came for Sunday dinner after church. And one time, my grandfather showed up on a Friday evening with a pimply-faced private he'd run into near the bus station while on his way home from work. Mother and Pell made the boy a pallet on the floor, and he spent the weekend. Then he got back on the bus and went off to do a grownup soldier's duty. I'm sure he had a surname, but afterward, we always just called him "Bill Gruber" for nearby Camp Gruber where he was stationed.

I've wondered from time to time if any of those brave youngsters ever thought as they went into battle of the fried chicken and biscuits and iced tea and the unqualified respect we served along with the food.

In Muskogee – probably in every small town in the country – you flew the flag on the Fourth of July. It was natural, it was unquestioned, it was like wearing the shiny paper poppies on Memorial Day. You just did it.

Then, in the decades following World War II, the country changed, and flag flying got complicated. It did for me, at least. Old truths of American life began to be replaced by turmoil, self-doubt, and conflict.

We looked up one day, and Bill Gruber had morphed into a faceless National Guardsman shooting down college students on a campus in Ohio.

Pell remained steadfast in her unquestioning love of the flag right through McCarthyism, political assassinations, Vietnam, and all the rest of it. When she was living out her time in the little apartment at Honor Heights, the brightest point in her day was seeing Old Glory raised every morning. (She never called the flag anything but Old Glory.) I was glad she had that certainty and good cheer in her life, but I thought she was overlooking some dark truths about our country.

Even now, I find it difficult to sit on the porch of my imposing house in Saranac Lake – it's almost exactly twelve times larger than the one in Muskogee where Bill Gruber slept on the floor that time – I find it difficult to look down at Lake Flower and the mountains beyond without thinking of the misery of many of the people living within a few blocks of my New York City apartment. This old house in the North Country and my blessed life in it is almost unimaginably far removed from that of the poor in New York City, who for whatever reasons, live desolate lives of squalor and pain in one of the richest and most civilized cities the earth has ever known. It's not fair.

I figure I get to sit on my porch and feel secure, financially and otherwise, in large measure because I'm lucky. Ann and I worked hard for this, but before all the work, we were lucky. We were born into loving families and nurtured on life-giving values, our choices along the way have been mostly good ones, and we've never known a day of not being intelligent, ambitious, and hopeful. We have received all the bounty of life in this country and none of the burden.

However all that may be, Pell would expect me to fly Old Glory today. And so I am. Pell died fifteen years ago, but at first light this morning, she and I marched across my front lawn, drums rolling, a bugle blowing, and we ran Old Glory up to its full thirty-foot height. This afternoon I'm taking four generations of her descendants to the village parade. In the evening, we'll watch the fireworks on Lake Flower. Sometime during the day, we're going to gather on the porch for a group photograph. While we're there, we'll sing without reservation "God Bless America."

 I guess the way it works is this: when you are blessed with Pell for a grandmother, and you saw Bill Gruber off to war, even if you get to be prosperous while many are in want, you take time out now and then from questions about fairness and the state of the nation.

Finally, a Big Christmas Tree
2003

This year, Ann and I set about realizing a long-held dream. We were, by God, going to have a Christmas right out of *It's a Wonderful Life*, one so chic and trendy it would make Martha Stewart envious, one that might have occurred in an English manor house during the late Victorian period. At the heart of it would be a BIG tree.

We had lived many years in Texas and other places that did not know real winter. Between us, we'd endured somewhere around seventy Christmases when it was up to sixty degrees too warm to snow. Not anymore. It was a foot deep outside the former monastery where we lived, and it was still coming down. Cold, too. Around zero every night.

In the past, we'd seldom had a fireplace, and "the stockings were hung from the doorjamb with care" had never quite satisfied. Well, that pitiable deprivation was behind us. Our historic residence in the Adirondacks had not one, but four, fireplaces. (Not enough. Later we would add a Franklin fireplace and an 1896 Glenwood parlor stove.) And ceilings high enough to accommodate a really tall tree, a tower of Christmas cheer.

I'd always preferred trees with long needles and dense with branches. Still do. Ann liked the kind with skinny little branches, spaced wide apart and the trunk plainly visible. Still does (she says). In a fit of Christmas good will, I agreed that for once we'd have her kind of tree. I promised myself that even if it didn't have but four or five branches and a total of ninety-one needles, I would spend the entire holidays saying, "My, what a beautiful tree." I pictured it in my mind as we sang "O Tannenbaum" on the way to the tree farm.

Ann's eye fell immediately on an Adirondack beauty the size of a small Sequoia with limbs remarkably dense and thick. It could hardly have been more different from the tree she said she'd always dreamed of but that I'd been too – I've forgotten whether the word was "stubborn" or "spoiled" – to agree to.

It took two strong men to move it to the trussing machine. They heaved and tugged mightily to get it to pass through. Branches snapped, and the air was filled with the sound of mechanical whining. The men grunted and swore oaths inappropriate to the season. At last, the thing emerged netted with many, many rounds of twine, but looking like it might burst its bonds at any minute.

The two trussers drafted another guy, and the three of them hoisted the brute up onto the top of the Suburban. I tied it on the best I could, but my fingers were too cold to do it properly. Onlookers muttered about how "seasonals" (a pejorative term for those of us who don't live in the Adirondacks year round) couldn't even tie a Christmas tree on top of a car. I think they were jealous. Anyway, we drove out with the tree barely hanging on.

I drove the several highway miles back to town at twenty miles an hour, telling myself that the cars behind were queued up there to see the magnificent thing home with proper ceremony.

In our driveway, I waved goodbye to the honor guard and got to work. I reached up to pry it off the car, and that's when I realized how heavy it was. (A more observant person would have put that together when a third man had to be drafted in order to put it up there.) It was fresh cut and full of sap, and besides that, much of the snow that had sat prettily on its stately, outstretched branches while it was on the lot, had been bound up inside. When a tree has a girth like that one did, it can hold a lot of snow.

I got its trunk over the edge of the luggage rack, and when critical mass was reached, the thing came down easily – right on top of me. Fortunately, the big rocks under the snow at the edge of the driveway did nothing really inconvenient, such as snap my spine, but the heavy end of the tree did have its way with my wrist.

I lay in the snow for a few minutes and pleaded with Ann to stop with the questions. "Are you hurt? Is it your back?" The tongue clucking, too.

I pulled my glove down a little and sneaked a look at the wound. It wasn't as serious as it felt. Once I poured out the pooled blood and tied on a Boy Scout tourniquet, I'd be fine. (The scar remains to this day.) Meanwhile, I could just leave my wrist in the snow and continue the numbing that had afflicted me all afternoon.

Ann, who was having back trouble, developed a sudden need for something from the grocery store and left me to deal with the thing on my own.

I had a plan. So I wouldn't have to pick it up, I would just slide it over the snow, up the steps, across the porch, and through the big front door.

Halfway there, I looked back on a trail of bloody needles, globs of dirty snow, and an angry chlorophyll smear. Hmm. It probably wasn't a good idea to drag it into the house and across the newly refinished floors, brushing as I went the hideously expensive and difficult-to-hang William Morris wallpaper that Ann had given such care to selecting. Better to leave it out on the porch and melt the bound-up snow with a hair dryer. I had never used a hairdryer. I didn't know that they blow warm air, not hot, and that they do it in a broad, diffuse pattern, not the bullet of heat that I needed.

After an hour or so, it came to me that it would be better to take the tree through the side door into the mudroom, which has a slate floor. There it would rest in state until the next day. I would put up a velvet rope to keep order among the throngs of villagers who would crowd in to view it. Overnight, the snow would melt, the thing would become lighter, I'd be able to move it easily, and I wouldn't drip sticky, melting snow all over the house.

I dragged it up the driveway a few inches at a time, leaving drops of blood on the needle-strewn snow, creating thereby a festive green and red pattern. I completed the journey from front porch to inside the mudroom in just under an hour.

I put doormats of various sizes and types in the middle of the floor. Using sandbags, a couple of sawhorses, and odd scraps of building materials, I managed to prop the tree in an upright position. (I can't recall why I thought that important. It surely wasn't.) I envisioned the thing neatly drip, drip, dripping onto the mats all through the night, while Ann and I slept the peaceful sleep of an honest squire and his lady. I turned the two nearby radiators to their highest levels and retired to administer first aid and start working on removal of pine resin from my hands. (Later I was told by the people at the Christmas tree farm that the best way to remove it is with peanut butter. I mean to try that next year.)

I got up a couple of times in the night and went down to see if the snow was melting. It was. A large and growing pool of nasty looking liquid was spreading steadily over the floor.

Next morning, I put on aggression along with my long underwear and gathered up tools.

Ann and I still had not come to an accurate understanding of how hostile and formidable the thing was. I confidently set out our family-treasure, cast-iron stand, WD 40 to persuade the rusty screws on the stand to turn, pliers, and gloves.

Ann said that we could just do what we did when removing a tree at the end of the season. We'd simply turn it on its side atop a sheet and slide it into the living room. There it would reside in majesty in the south-facing bow window until Epiphany, all the while shining its benison of colorful light down the hill onto the Burger King customers wending their holiday way through the drive-through line.

IN PASSING. SCENES FROM AN UNCONVENTIONAL LIFE

First, though, I would need to reduce the circumference of the trunk so that it would fit into the family-treasure, cast-iron stand. Shouldn't take long. I got my hatchet.

I wrestled the thing back outside. Never mind that it was sixteen degrees out there, and the mudroom was already such a mess, I wouldn't have made it much worse by doing the work inside.

At least it wasn't difficult to get it out. Once over the threshold, it shot down the slippery steps like an Olympic luge and came to rest on the ice field below.

My plan was to hold it up with one hand and chop away at the base with my other. (I suppose all that cold weather had diminished my ability to think straight.)

The hatchet didn't look like much – a consequence of being left out in the yard one autumn and not being seen again until the snow melted in late April. It wasn't very sharp either. But I wasn't about to go to the hardware store for a file. Then I'd have to buy a vise to hold it and a work bench to mount the vice on and no telling what else. I was more than a year into renovation efforts before I realized the importance of staying focused and not getting distracted by ancillary projects. That way lay endless trips to the hardware store.

On the ice, I could hardly keep my feet, much less hold up a giant Christmas tree while whacking away at its trunk with a dull hatchet. I tried leaning it against the house, but it was no more able to stand on the ice than I was. It slid down, almost severing the tiptop that was perfect for holding a star. I had carefully measured the height of the tree, including the phallus, to be sure that the star would almost, but not quite, touch the ceiling. I lashed the tip back on with fishing line.

Just as full-body frostbite began to set in, I succeeded in whittling down the tree's base. I drilled a hole for the stand's spike and dragged the thing back up the steps and into the mudroom.

Ann came in with a sheet. She'd been busy all morning wrapping gifts. She likes wrapping gifts, and I'm glad. It had kept her occupied while I slipped and fell repeatedly on the ice as I whacked at the tree's trunk. Had she not been thus occupied, I'm pretty sure she would have pointed out that I was in danger of chopping off my leg – a job even a dull axe could manage. (Ann and I differ in our tolerance of risk.)

We rolled the thing onto the sheet, and away we went, bound for the living room. Nothing to it.

There I got my legs under me and heaved the giant up and into the family-treasure, cast-iron stand. If it had been a single ounce heavier, I could not have done it. But there it stood, straight and promising and still straining at its fetters like a rodeo bronc, quivering and wild-eyed, waiting for the chute to open. All that remained before putting on the ornaments was to cut the heavy twine that kept it from expanding to its full majestic girth.

Starting at the top, we cut, and branches sprang open, happy as kids on the last day of school. Then, about halfway down, the remaining intact strings exploded and unraveled all at once. Every remaining branch popped out angrily, spraying snow and ice wall to wall, floor to ceiling. The thing had been no more willing to thaw than a Christmas turkey. In no time at all, puddles of ugly goop began forming around where the tree lay on its side.

Ann ran for towels, and I again heaved the thing into the stand. Once again it fell down; the stand had too little circumference to hold it up. Even if it could have, I'd been too cold to reduce the size of the trunk enough so that it was possible to pour water into the receptacle. Water would be essential. Epiphany was a long way off, and until then, the tree would reside in stately elegance midway between the life-threatening dryness of a nine-foot-long radiator and the biggest fireplace in the house.

We considered the situation as we watched the snow that had refused to melt while in the mudroom turn into sticky little gray-green pools on the newly finished maple floors of the living room. We thought and thought. A guy wire attached to the ceiling? Over my dead body (not, it seemed, that hard to come by). New sheetrock had been installed there twice already. A guy wire to the radiator? Yes, but there was nothing else to attach one to, and a single guy wire would be no help. Make a stand out of a washtub full of sand? That would be outstandingly decorative, though a little new-agey for my taste. Anyway, I wouldn't be able to lift the tree high enough to get it into a tub.

We needed help. Father Dan across the street, was both a priest and a triathlete. Just the man for the job, but he wasn't home. Neither was David next door. Neighbor Brian had a bad back. Oh well, even a seasonal ought to be able to put up a Christmas tree without sending out for help.

Ann swept wet, sticky needles into piles, aggravating her back condition, and I sucked them up with a Shop-Vac, and we discussed various solutions, and – well – we bickered.

I thought we should take the thing out onto the front porch and leave it there till we could come up with a plan. Or maybe someone would steal it. That would solve our problem nicely. Ann was of the clenched-jaw opinion that the solarium was the proper place. We only argue over important matters. Especially at Christmas.

In keeping with the magic of the season, Ann came up with a new idea: a bright, shiny Christmas vision that was a variation on my idea.

"Let's *leave* it out on the porch for the whole season. We can attach it to the porch swing's eyebolt with a wire. Put outdoor lights on it. And then get a more manageable tree for inside."

"Great idea," I said. Actually, that had been my plan all along.

On the drive back to the city, Ann decided she'd been rash.

"That's such a fine fat tree, let's keep it inside."

"Fine with me," I said. Actually, that had been my plan all along.

"We'll just buy an extra-large stand," she said with finality.

During the week, we found a stand that attached to a four-foot-square piece of plywood and had a large reservoir. Problem solved.

And so it came to pass that at dusk on Christmas Eve, we received a miracle. With snow falling dreamily and angels singing to beat the band, we stood with our backs to the fireplace and admired the BIG Christmas tree we had always wanted. It was beautiful. We felt blessed and contented and most of all – this is the Christmas miracle – we felt free – free not to have to put up a BIG Christmas tree *ever again*.

The Trouble with My Porch Swing 2004

Warm summer days, a sprawling Victorian house in the mountains, a long, deep verandah, and a porch swing. Bliss. Trouble was, to enjoy the swing, I had to do battle with a billion-dollar corporation. I hadn't expected that.

* * * *

Scarcely anyone has a porch swing anymore. Most houses don't have the kind of porch where you can hang a swing. My guess is millions of Americans have never sat in one and never felt the slowed-pulse contentment of gently moving back and forth in a summer breeze. But never mind that – the porch swing lives on. It has outlasted the arrival of air conditioning, television, Levittowns, and McMansions. Mostly in the mind, of course, but it's no less real for that. Lots of very important things exist in the mind. Or maybe the heart. Somewhere inside. Anger, envy, and greed, for example. But also peace, stillness, and calm.

Those last are the essence of the porch swing. They are the reason the porch swing construct has endured, even as porches and swings themselves have become rare.

I actually do have a porch swing, and it is dear to me.

When Ann and I first saw the monastery, the front porch had been enclosed to create bedrooms, so I doubt we visualized in much detail the porch we have now – a deep, open, seventy-foot-long sweep, furnished during the short Adirondack summer with wicker furniture and rocking chairs, the railing hung with boxes of snapdragons and geraniums, and down near the end where honeysuckle and lilacs rise up from outside, a three-person swing. We didn't see all that, but I have no doubt that it registered in some way. The house has proved to be strong and mysterious – easily capable of projecting a vision we were not immediately aware of.

Porch swings may have more power now that they are rare. There's a good chance they went relatively unnoticed a hundred years ago when people lived lives that were quieter in almost every way. Maybe that's a romantic reinvention of the past, but I don't think so. Without traffic jams, TSA inspections, nuclear weapons, smartphones, hedge funds, the Tea Party, Al-Qaeda, the neighbor's Sunday afternoon chain saw, and extended colloquies with tech support in Mumbai, life must surely have been calmer, less annoying, less scattered and threatening. In such a way of being, porch swings probably didn't call attention to themselves the way they do now.

I'm grateful to have a porch swing, because in it, on a good day, I can more or less comply with the Psalmist's useful suggestion to "be still and know that I am God."

The trouble is, good days have been hard to come by. For several years, it has been possible to realize the promise of my swing only before 7:00 a.m. That's when a loudspeaker about 150 feet down the hill begins bawling, "**WELCOME TO BURGER KING. MAY I TAKE YOUR ORDER, PLEASE?**" Over and over, all day long, until past my bedtime. It kind of takes the pleasure out of porch sitting.

Before we bought the house, the nuns disclosed that occasionally they'd been moved to ask the manager to lower the volume. We too did that for a time. The hamburger people would turn it down, but then for some reason, after a few days or weeks, it would go loud again, and I'd head back down the hill. Still, we managed to live together in moderate comity.

But after a year or so of this mildly inconvenient back and forth, the local human who owned the franchise sold it to Carrols Corporation, an outfit that owned or managed hundreds of fast-food establishments.

IN PASSING. SCENES FROM AN UNCONVENTIONAL LIFE

That caused a lot of trouble. Before long, the speaker noise went from annoyance, petty and sporadic to aural assault, severe and frequent.

Early in the Carrols era – before the corporate version of the noise nuisance became both intolerable and deeply strange – I went down to ask for help on a different problem. The lights over their parking lot glared up onto the front of our house where the many-windowed master bedroom was situated. Going to bed was like facing a B-movie interrogation. I put up with it a long time before I dared seek relief. I figured they'd probably dismiss my complaint as anti-business liberalism, I'd get mad, and we'd yell at each other. I'd about as soon contract Lyme disease. But one night when I couldn't find my sleep mask and had to make do with a folded towel over my eyes, I snapped. Next morning, down I went.

"Hi. I'm your neighbor up there in the former monastery," I said, pointing to the house. Over the next few years, I would always approach them with that line. I thought it well crafted in several ways.

"Neighbor" was disarming in that it suggested a community of interest (incorrectly, of course, but it was worth a try). Reminding them that the structure in question was the former monastery was another sneaky bit of cleverness. It was likely that some of the employees were Catholics, since a majority of the local population was. And I was always running into men who had been altar boys at monastery Masses and women who had been special friends of the nuns. If hamburger person was one of them, the likelihood of cooperation was much increased. My use of "up" offered still another subliminal suggestion (correctly in this instance) that would work in our favor. Ann and I were above; hamburger hell was below.

Continuing to be crafty, I switched to a diffident, I'd-be-ever-so-grateful tone.

"Do you suppose you could change the angle of your parking lot's lights so that they aren't pointed up at my bedroom windows?"

"No problem," the manager answered.

No problem? Jerk. He was obviously messing with me.

But he wasn't. Coincidentally, the corporation was at that very moment planning to install a new lighting system that would direct the light more down, less up.

Life was good.

But as it turned out, not all that good.

Stay with me now. I'm closing in on an enigma that is central to this tale of North Country conflict.

In due time, Carrols Corporation did change the parking lot lighting. While they were at it, they installed a new drive-through audio system – a loud one. Severely loud. It could be heard a block away. Maybe farther. Oh well, I'd just go down and ask these new neighbors to turn it down, like I'd done when the business was owned by a human.

The guy at the counter looked like he could be cooperative. Nothing about him suggested that he wanted to force us to sell the monastery and go back where we came from.

I made my well-crafted request.

The look on his face seemed apologetic. And more. Something hard to make out. Like he was about to say something that was simultaneously true and preposterous. He was.

"We *can't* turn it down."

I thought he meant he was not allowed to turn it down. That was not what he meant.

"It doesn't have a volume control."

I gave up on talking and stared at walls for a while. On one of them, a plastic sign invited customers to take up any problems with Bob, the District Manager. Well, I had a problem, so I wrote down District Manager Bob's phone number and walked back up the little hill to my wonderful house with the grand porch that looks down on hamburger hell and the lake and across the lake to the distant mountains. On the way, I thought about what it must be like to work for a company that does not allow a local manager sufficient autonomy to be able to control speaker volume. But I didn't get too worked up. At that point, I was still pretty sure that District Manager Bob and I could work it out.

District Manager Bob, whose office was fifty miles away in Plattsburgh, explained some things to me. When a car drove up, it tripped a sensor that set off a recorded greeting, the "**WELCOME TO BURGER KING. MAY I TAKE YOUR ORDER, PLEASE**?" that was beginning to go around in my head like the ringing of tinnitus. And the guy at the counter had told me the truth. The volume of the greeting could not be controlled at the local level. However, the words that followed the taped greeting, words such as, "you want fries with that?" were performed live, and from that point on, volume could be adjusted. That squared with my experience. It was usually just the greeting that tormented me on the porch. Or in my bed, if I hadn't gotten up early. I usually didn't hear, "What size?" or "What's happening, dude?" or anything else the person inside said to the customer in the car.

I speculated that someone in burger central had determined the ideal volume for the greeting. No doubt a lot of money had gone into research, and focus groups had been convened in order to arrive at it. Some assistant vice-president had probably been honored with a really swell framed document that designated him "Decibel Man of the Year."

We have now arrived at the central mystery foretold a few paragraphs back. Once the perfect volume was ascertained and the greeter was anointed accordingly, it became impossible for *anyone*, not just local employees – *anyone* – to change it.

Being an obtuse person, I said to District Manager Bob, "Why?"

I can't remember the precise wording of his answer. Probably because it was so strange. Something about the speaker being controlled by a computer. And there was a chip involved in some way. He seemed to suggest that the greeter therefore had a soul, a will, existed in the great beyond, and was unreachable by ordinary mortals.

Nevertheless, good-man Bob, District Manager, reluctantly agreed to call in a technician from Albany, 150 miles away, to have a go at adding volume control. Let me point out that Carrols Corporation at that time had annual revenues of around a billion dollars. Something about that level of commercial power and not being able to adjust the volume on a loudspeaker just didn't match up.

As District Manager Bob expected, the techie from Albany was unable to bring the thing to heel. (I wondered if he knew the factory-trained inspector who had looked at the malfunctioning fifty-year-old boiler in the monastery and for $350 pointed out that it was old. He too was from Albany.)

I went back to District Manager Bob to discuss this unsatisfactory outcome. He gave me to understand that the company had at that point spent several hundred dollars in an effort to turn down the volume and be a good neighbor, and he implied that they had reached the limit of how much they would invest in it. Now, I'm neither a hamburger executive nor a techie, but I speedily figured out a cheap and easy solution. I offered it to District Manager Bob free of charge.

"Look, Bob. Since it's a computer that's causing this difficulty, here's what you do. Just go up to the first person you see who has zits and offer the kid a week of burgers to bring the computerized greeter under human control. In less time than it takes to slap together a Whopper®, you'll be able to move the volume from loud to soft and all points in between."

District Manager Bob rejected my excellent solution. I could hear condescension in his voice. No matter what his actual words were, I heard, "Paul, you don't understand the hamburger business. Leave this to the experts."

My annoyance was piling up like a Saranac Lake snow drift. The Carrols Corporation had effectively kicked me off my own porch. Then, as I was musing about what Gandhi would have done if he'd gotten worked up about a tough problem such as the noise from hamburger hell rather than the relatively easy one of how to run the English out of India, a promising turn of events took place.

The corporation offered to sell the franchise to District Manager Bob. Bob was ready to retire, but the price was too good to turn down. He would move to Saranac Lake and spend his golden years there grilling burgers and frying fries within spitting distance of my house. And wanting to be a good neighbor and village resident, he would redouble his efforts to lower the volume.

One sunny morning a short time later, I discovered former District Manager Bob, now Franchisee Bob, and Mrs. Bob at my front door. They wanted to try out the swing and gauge for themselves how serious the problem was. After a few minutes of easy swinging, they looked at each other and nodded in silent agreement. "I wouldn't want to have to listen to that either," Franchisee Bob said, as Mrs. Bob continued nodding in agreement. I thought their attitude surprisingly empathetic. To them, the squawking greeter must have sounded like the jingle of the cash register. I was grateful that they could imagine what it sounded like to me. So I offered up a sop of reasonableness.

"Look, Bob, our interests are not in conflict. I know you can find a way to make the greeting loud enough for you to earn a living and at the same time quiet enough so I don't hear it." I wanted to say, "You can turn that damned thing down to where I can't hear it, and the morons who drive up there to order will still be able to poison themselves, and you'll still be able to make a living in your chosen field of being an enemy of good health." I rejected that approach as possibly provocative.

He promised to try to find a way to control the volume. Mrs. Bob increased the pace of her nodding. And Bob allowed that, as Franchisee, he would be more able to accomplish that extremely difficult – indeed, till now impossible – task. We shook hands, and I was filled with hope that one day before I died – actuarial tables gave me a good twenty years – the front porch of my beautiful old house in an Adirondack village would be free of burger torment.

Not long after that, I set about to make a strong gesture of goodwill to Franchisee Bob and Mrs. Bob. I would buy and eat a Whopper® with cheese. Maybe even a Double Whopper® Sandwich Meal. I was that grateful.

Mrs. Bob was behind the counter.

"Hi. Thank you again for working with me on this problem. It's very neighborly of you." I meant it, too.

"You're welcome, but we're not staying. We've sold the franchise back to the corporation."

I changed my mind about having a Whopper®.

Good-man Bob and his wife had only owned it a few weeks, but that was all it took for them to realize that Saranac Lake was too far from their grandchildren, who lived an hour away. That seemed implausible to me. More likely, the reason probably had something to do with the speaker.

Anyway, they left, and Ann and I were still one with hamburger orders. (That probably bothered her even more than me; she had been a vegetarian for more than two decades.)

I wasn't sure what to do next, but I thought it might be informative to investigate a little. I got in my car and drove up to the speaker like I was going to buy a burger, so I could see how loud it was to a customer. Too loud. I asked friends to go through the line. They agreed with me. It was punk-rock loud. To me that didn't seem like a smart sales tactic. It called into question the widespread belief that corporations are efficient and that they act in their self-interest.

Battle weary though I was, I got in touch with the new guy, District Manager Pete, also working out of Plattsburgh. He suggested that we have a meeting. But he was often on the road, and I was frequently in New York City, so it was some time before we met. When we did, it was by chance.

I kept meaning to take my problem to some powerful and perhaps sympathetic person in corporate headquarters. But before I would get around to it, Ann and I would find ourselves back home in New York City. There, comfortably swaddled in the sound of jackhammers, dump-truck engine braking, car alarms, and such, I didn't have much stomach for simultaneously combating noise that was three hundred miles away.

Anyway, while waiting for something to develop from my overtures to District Manager Pete, I tried to adjust my attitude. I was probably making too much of the problem. After all, in effect, the barrage of **"WELCOME TO BURGER KING. MAY I TAKE YOUR ORDER, PLEASE?"** often lasted only an hour or so. On a fine day, by around eight, it began to come and go in intensity, sometimes singing solo, sometimes accompanied by other racket, and sometimes completely covered up by a full chorus of more powerful rivals. The awful whole truth is the Burger King greeter was but one of many pernicious sounds that debased the quality of my porch life.

Ever-increasing numbers of personal watercraft made an angry buzzing noise as they circled around and around on the lake just across the street from the Burger King.

And on one festive weekend each year, hordes of Harley-Davidson riders swarmed through Saranac Lake en route to Tupper Lake, a hard-scrabble village thirty miles to the southwest, where they would enjoy nature and bump up the sales of Slim Jims and beer. Many of the hogs were altered to be super rumbly in the sure and certain belief that the louder the sound, the longer the penis, a bodily feature many men will do just about anything to achieve, including broadcasting roaring and popping sounds over county-size patches of America.

The situation became even more unpleasant when the noise of those short-dick sons of bitches was joined by the tooth-rattling bass from boom cars lined up for burgers.

Oh yeah, and a seaplane occasionally made an ear-splitting landing and takeoff out among the jet skis. (It seemed to present a safety issue, but I was not especially concerned.)

When two über-loud airboats took up residence on the lake, they retired the noxious-noise trophy.

In the context, burger noise was small beer. Still, it remained my primary source of irritation. I had done battle with the perpetrators and lost, and I hate losing.

Then one morning as I was walking across the Burger King parking lot, something most unexpected happened. Like winning the lottery. As the first car of the day eased to a stop in the drive-through lane, a well-modulated, smiling voice wafted from the speaker. "May I take your order, please?" I hotfooted through the door like a gymnast approaching a vaulting horse.

The woman behind the counter didn't know what was going on with the speaker, just that they were no longer using the automatic greeter. She couldn't say whether it was broken or Carrols had changed its policy or if some other explanation applied. She did say she thought a human-to-human interaction made for a better hamburger experience. Channeling Mrs. Bob, I nodded enthusiastically in agreement. Then without prompting and without her knowing how much I had longed to hear the words that followed, she said, "we can control the volume now."

I launched excitedly into a rapid-fire, spit-flinging recital of my history with the issue. I was hardly well started when she interrupted me. "Would you like to talk with the District Manager? He's in the building."

I sure did.

District Manager Pete told me that after I had contacted him, he'd written a letter to Carrols Corporation suggesting that they get rid of the automatic greeter, since it disturbed the neighbors. Burger central agreed and replaced it with one that had a volume control. Pete seemed like a better District Manager than Bob.

For the next year or two, the problem was less burdensome. We returned to the earlier pattern in which I asked them to lower the volume when it got too loud, and they'd accommodate me, and after a bit it would spike again, and so on.

Finally, the conflict went away altogether; Carrols Corporation closed up shop. The building sat empty for a time, then it was turned into a restaurant that did not have a drive-through lane and a fiendish loudspeaker. The battle was over.

Even so, sometimes, I still hear the raucous cry of hamburger commerce the way amputees feel pain in limbs they no longer have. If these phantom sounds ever stop tormenting me, I may take on the jet skis and those cursed airboats.

Winter Nights in the Monastery 2016

This former monastery is a good house for winter sleeping. It hasn't always been this way.

Before we got new improved valves on the radiators, they would sing like tea kettles unless they were periodically bled of air. Since there is at least one radiator in every room, it took a long time to do that. And too often, the operation would make a substantial contribution to my hypertension.

I'd open a little valve (known somewhat informally as a "pisser valve") with a gadget that looks like a skate key and hold a pan under it to catch the slight stream of hot water that would without warning gush out when all of the trouble-making air had been released. Just a turn or two would start the process. More than that, and the valve would come apart, and a piece of it would fall into some place almost totally inaccessible. After I finally recovered it, it had to be fitted back on in the stream of hot water. Not scalding hot, but hot enough to be uncomfortable – you wouldn't put your hand in it if you didn't have to. As I worked and cussed, nasty water stained beyond redemption swaths of new carpet.

Bleeding radiators was tedious – like scraping old paint or removing shower grout. I would attempt to get it over with quickly by opening several valves at the same time. That could work in theory, but in practice it was problematic. In the first place, the containers that caught the water had to be big enough to allow for the occasional larger-than-usual flow. Too big, and they wouldn't fit in the spot where the flow would hit them. To my regret, I'd sometimes take a chance on a smaller one.

With three or four open and relieving themselves at the same time, things would get a little tense. A fair amount of running from room to room would ensue. Even so, the drama was often not compelling enough to keep me focused, and I would sometimes forget about one. Left open, the flow could continue – potentially – until the village water supply ran dry. On one occasion, a wall and part of a ceiling in a room below had to be repainted.

After a couple of years of doing this dance, I began to neglect radiator maintenance, and night-time whistling became a part of life in this house. Finally, we installed automatic bleeders. They have improved my life generally and contributed to peaceful sleeping specifically.

There are, however, other night sounds, which have yet to be successfully addressed. For several years, squirrels have been having a party in the rafters between the ceiling of the master bedroom and the floor above. Why they picked that spot, I don't know. They have lots and lots of other choices. But they did pick it, and it's like having a garage band up there.

No matter what barriers are erected, in a cold climate squirrels will find a way into warm houses the way snowbirds go to Florida. When neighbor Peter discovered a hole in a soffit, he replaced it, and in no time, the squirrels gnawed a new hole.

Usually, they winter in an attic. That's not such a problem. They can be trapped or killed easily in an attic. But as I said, at my house they're not in the attic, they're between the second and third floors directly over our bed.

The obvious way to deal with them would be to find where they get in and put up a barrier made of something they couldn't gnaw through, such as diamonds. But that would probably be no more effective than Trump's Great Wall; they'd still find a way in. Anyway, we haven't been able to find the entry point.

IN PASSING. SCENES FROM AN UNCONVENTIONAL LIFE

Last year, we employed a hired gun. The guy stepped out of his pickup, pulling on serious-looking gloves, casting a baleful eye up the side of the house, looking as fearless as a new Marshall who'd been called in to make hash of a bunch of outlaws. His first move was the same as that of all nuisance-animal specialists; he took a close look under the eaves.

In our case, that meant climbing a ladder that extended up through the clouds to a point where the air is thin. Two kinds of people – both deranged – will perform that act; those who have no Workers' Compensation insurance (unthinkably risky) and those who do have insurance (unthinkably expensive). We saved up and hired one of the latter. He failed to solve the problem.

We turned to Google, where we learned that sprinkling moth flakes around the attic was the preferred remedy. (Are we the only people whose squirrel problem is not in the attic?) We tried to learn from it, even if the suggested solution was not exactly on point.

Apparently, squirrels don't like moth flakes. It was unclear what their dislike was based on. Not smell. The instructions called for odorless flakes so as not to stink up the house. Did the squirrels eat the moth flakes, then? Get sick and die? Dead squirrels in the attic would smell worse than moth flakes, and no one would recommend that. Anyway, I doubt if a squirrel would eat moth flakes. To this day, my questions remain unanswered.

The moth-flake treatment is reminiscent of the defense I once tried against lawn-destroying skunks. The way to make skunks stay over in your neighbor's yard is to spread fox urine around. It's available for purchase online. Naturally, the mind turns to methods of collection. Doesn't sound like a very good job to me. And one hears poor little Jimmy explaining at school that his daddy makes his living collecting fox piss. It comes in dried form, too.

Back to our squirrel problem. We got contractor/caretaker John to open up a couple of spots that seemed to be on the route into the master bedroom ceiling and sprinkle moth flakes there. It had no effect. Maybe moth flakes are effective only against *attic* squirrels.

Mercifully, the squirrel problem is not constant. Lately, we've had some fairly long stretches without them disturbing our sleep. The best I can figure, that's because we've had an exceptionally mild winter up till now, and they're happy to play outside, demonstrating thereby that global warming is not totally objectionable.

Not seeing as many mice this year either. That, too, makes for better sleeping. Normally, they start finding their way inside around Halloween. From then until spring, Baby Kitty pounces on them down in the pantry then brings them up live and struggling to our bedroom to play with them and torture them before killing and eating the good parts. It's a grisly business punctuated by BK's galloping pursuit and pitiful mouse squeaks.

In this warm year, there has been less of that. But to stay in shape, BK plays noisily with her toy mouse, and the sound is about the same as during a normal winter. Just no cries for mercy.

Other night sounds are of unknown etiology. Some people find them scary; others, interesting. They strike me as in the natural order of things; the old house is alive, and it murmurs from time to time. What it's saying, though, is not clear. Less fancifully, strong winds can move the house around a little – not much, but enough to cause old joints to rub and creak. Nothing unusual about that.

The living room and dining room have maple floors. Walk across them after they've not known footsteps for a while, and they creak and talk. Not only directly underfoot either; all around the room. It's a kind of grumbling sound. The first few times that happened, we were sleeping in the bedroom that is directly above. We suspected an intruder, but we never discovered anyone, so we don't remark it much anymore.

Most likely, it's one of the nuns who lived here in peace and even in death will not leave. They are welcome, and so are their angelic footsteps. I don't understand how incorporeal beings can make sounds, but in the season just past, we were reminded that archangel Gabriel had a conversation with the Virgin Mary, and an angel spoke to some shepherds, and other angels sang "glory to God in the highest." So, it seems plausible that our deceased ladies make sounds.

We've been using the fireplaces more during this mild winter. With less boiler-generated heat being sucked up the chimney, wood fires with the dampers open are less expensive, and we enjoy them more often. It has been a little challenging, though. We didn't plan well, the supply of seasoned firewood is running low, and we have to burn some that's still a little green. To enjoy a respectable fire requires a combination of a good initial blaze of dry wood and later adding green that has been split into smaller-than-usual pieces. (Ann is pretty good at splitting logs – a real North Country girl about it. She refuses, however, to wear Carhartts. I don't know why.)

But once the fire is right, good whisky or tea is in hand, chairs are positioned just so, Baby Kitty is on one lap or the other, life takes on storybook peacefulness that segues easily into sound sleep. It's six medium-size steps from the bedroom hearth to the bed. Then, if incidental noises are noticed at all, they're mostly acceptable, some even welcome. In either case, until the snowplow scrapes by just before first light, the monastery night is ruled by the cold-climate, mammalian urge to get into a warm place and sleep until spring.

Frame of Reference
2016

The John Ford movie, *The Searchers*, opens with a shot that looks from inside a house, through a doorway onto a vast western landscape in which a lone rider approaches. The doorway serves as a picture frame; it limits and forms what is seen and experienced.

In recent years, much has been made of the metaphorical frame in political discourse. Placing issues in a frame limits counter arguments. Abortion, for example, is framed as either right-to-life or freedom-to-choose, pro-life or pro-choice.

The frame itself often goes unremarked. I don't recall what kind of door is in *The Searchers*, but whatever it is, it shapes the reality of the lone rider approaching. Imagine looking out through a portal of ornately carved wood or a sixteen-pane window rimed with frost or the crude opening of a sod house or an opening covered by a translucent curtain. In each case, what is seen beyond is partly formed by the frame.

From my desk, I look through a doorway out onto a cure porch of the former sanatorium and beyond that to five-story-tall conifers and a few box elders and other deciduous trees and beyond that, during bare-tree winter, to the cemetery and beyond that to the road that exists dimly during the day and as winking car lights in the dark.

The opening is wide enough to allow the passage of a hospital bed, an appropriately large size for an aperture that is bordered by many defining artifacts of my life.

On the far edge of my desk are small stand-up photographs. Everything out past them lines up above their tops. I can focus on the pictures or on what is beyond, but not on both at the same time.

On the left, is a nude shot of twenty-seven-year-old Ann perched on a rock in the rapids of the Pedernales River, smiling into the camera, at once innocent and glowing with carnal promise. A pair of photos from two or three years later show her at a kitchen table being a young wife. Next to her, my father and I are standing by the new 1948 Mercury that replaced the old Plymouth for which parts were hard to find during the war. Then my maternal grandmother and her brother pose as children for a studio portrait in about 1897, which happens to be the same year that fifteen hundred miles to the north of where they posed, men were building the house in which the photo now hangs. Next to them, my infant mother is in her cowboy father's arms on a horse in 1913. He seems to be taking a break from working cattle.

The desktop is cluttered. Hardly enough room to work sometimes. I don't like to put things away. That's how they get lost. I prefer having stacks of papers and files out in plain sight and within arm's reach.

My friends Jack and Jim have spent little time in the presence of my desk, not this one or others. That's providential. I've seen theirs; maybe a computer keyboard or a pen that escaped being put where it belongs, but otherwise just bare wood without even dust on it. My way would probably make them queasy. Nevertheless, it's who I am; my clutter and photos are part of my frame of reference.

More photos and some artwork hang on the walls that surround the door. On the side of the chimney are pen-and-ink drawings from the sketchbook of my old friend, Walle. They're his vision of a gathering on Aransas Bay in Texas where we have been going for decades to fish and mess about in boats with friends.

On the radiator cover to the right of the door, there's a touched-up photo of my great-grandfather at, I guess, about age twenty. He was born in 1871. I was sixteen when he died. I had plenty of opportunities to get him to tell me about his life. When was the first time he saw an automobile? Did he have any books as a child? What was it like to have a toothache in those days? I didn't ask. Now it's too late.

IN PASSING. SCENES FROM AN UNCONVENTIONAL LIFE

I'm thinking I'll force my grandchildren to listen to me go on about my life before they were born. I could write it down, of course. I enjoy writing. But judging by the universal rejection of the memoir I wrote about renovating this old house, I conclude that I'm not much good at that kind of writing. Anyway, if I just speak my memories to the children, they will have a bigger role in creating the stories than if they read them. After their recollections of my maunderings fade, they'll get to add color and point of view and make up bits to fill in blanks. Is it too fanciful to think that I will thus have achieved a dollop of immortality? Maybe not.

On the wall above great-grandfather Pappy's photo is a reproduction of a 16th century drawing of Thomas Cranmer and associates gathered around a table compiling the Anglican Book of Common Prayer. Thoroughly Presbyterian Pappy would not want to be in close proximity to those Popish clerics. Oh well. Change happens, Pappy.

On the same wall are mementos of my writing; a poster advertising a stage adaptation of my novella, *A Franklin Manor Christmas;* a batik that comments wryly on the frustrations of trying to get published; a photo of my beloved cat, Peewee, falling asleep on my computer as I was working diligently to earn the National Book Award that's lost in the mail.

Beyond the door, out on the cure porch, is more definition, more me. Leaning against the frame of a window is a watercolor of an Adirondack scene, a gift from my friends, Mary and Mark. It speaks of my life in this place where I never imagined living and the friendships that have come with it. A tabletop, like my desk, is cluttered. It's mostly stacks of books that I look into periodically. (If they were on shelves, they'd be harder to locate, since the shelves are not very orderly.) Essays by E.B. White; collections of newspaper columns by the Texas writer Leon Hale; a Bible on top of an *Interpreters One-Volume Commentary on the Bible*; a *Webster's Third New International Dictionary*. Also, notes, drafts and half-finished efforts to transform some evanescent something into words on paper.

People who have had near-death experiences say that at the final moment, their whole life passed before their eyes like an old-fashioned newsreel, perceivable despite running at an unfathomably fast speed.

I would not like to review my *whole* life. I would much prefer a selection of images from among the good parts, the reconciling parts – something like what I see from my desk.

IN PASSING. SCENES FROM AN UNCONVENTIONAL LIFE

An Adirondack Evening in Late Autumn 2016

One day a couple of weeks after the election of Trump, the temperature here was unseasonably warm, increasing thereby the slack-jawed dismay the election had generated. So, the snow that began the next day and continued for over forty-eight hours was more welcome than the first snow usually is. It suggested that something approaching "normal" might yet be possible. After a soothing supper of autumn vegetable soup, I made a fire in the cast-iron stove of my upstairs study and settled down for an evening of reading.

BK the cat discovered the fire and my lap before I was well started. She and I went through bits of this book and that – whatever I could reach without standing up and disturbing her. Anyway, all I wanted was something to help me read my way back from the dismay generated by the election outcome.

At some point, I found a copy of *The Times Literary Supplement*. The articles in it often don't interest me or they are too learned. Not on that first-snow evening by the fire, though. Nick Groom, someone I'd never heard of, reviewed three books on the British experience of nature, and I was off into one of those altered states that happen sometimes when you read.

For a while, nothing existed in my world except the words, the fire, the falling snow (illuminated by floodlights high up under the eaves), and BK. The common expression for this experience is to "get lost" in a book. Not to be quarrelsome, but that's not what happens; in moments of intense reading, you get found, or at least you make progress in finding your way and you are reassured that you are on course. Getting lost is frightening; getting found is restorative. The latter is what I experienced that evening.

After a bit, Ann joined us. She and I don't often sit together in my study, but that evening she knew it was the best place to be of the many choices available. ("Just the two of you in that big house?") Actually, it was not so much a choice as a compulsion, the same as it was with me. The house has a way of ordering us around like that.

I don't recall what she was reading, but she was absorbed by it. Now and again, she would read something aloud to me or offer a response to some idea she'd come across. It was a little annoying; I was rambling among the hedgerows of England, reflecting on British ways of land use and property rights. But then I would encounter a phrase or an idea I just had to read to her, no doubt eliciting the same response. The interruptions were of small import though. I mention them here just for the purpose of realistic fullness.

For the most part, we spent the evening in companionable silence, a state that comes occasionally to couples who have earned it by years of being together, celebrating the good parts, overlooking the bad, and muddling through the quotidian. Such moments cannot be called into being by effort of will; they just happen. It helps, of course, to be sitting by a crackling fire with the wind making a racket and the first snow of the year whirling about and a good cat offering a model of calmness.

One of the reviews by Nick Groom was especially forceful, irresistible even, in its invitation to another place. The book was *The Running Hare, The Secret Life of Farmland* by John Lewis-Stempel. The review is not so much critique as story, chock full of British vocabulary and usage. It does, however, focus carefully on the book's argument for farming without chemicals. Groom charmingly calls it "a statement in weeds and wheat." In that same mode, he points out about conventional farming that "every time one buys the lie of cheap food, a flower or a bird dies."

I judge whether what I'm reading is worthwhile by the number of notes I take and words I look up. No notes, no unfamiliar or interesting words – little reason to continue. Groom's review resulted in a desktop cluttered with notes on scratch paper, suggesting (slightly) the accumulating snow.

Note: "Rootling." Rooting? Etymology.

Lewis-Stempel buys fifteen acres for his ideal wheat farm. Note. "Is that enough land to be commercially viable – or is it just an experimental plot?

Note. The place is named "Flinders." Is it customary in England to give a name to fifteen-acre patches? Does "Flinders" have some special significance?

Note. Lewis-Stempel plants by using a "seed fiddle." What's that?

And when someone writes as gracefully as Nick Groom does, it begs for information about who he is and how he became such an artful writer. It turns out he's a professor of English at the University of Exeter, information that sent me off on one of those side trips that makes reading fuller than what's before your eyes on the page.

Exeter is Willcott breeding ground. When I lived in London, I drove out there to see some family graves in a churchyard, but they had been bombed out during the war. I let my thoughts run along that path for a few minutes then went on to something else.

Page after page, snow kept falling, BK kept sleeping, companionable silence kept offering its benison. Then the fire died down, and we went to bed.

Sunday Matters

Bananas

Some Sunday mornings, I spend half an hour or more thinking about bananas. I do that when the preaching doesn't reach me. If the clergyperson exhorts me to behave in ways that are by God meet and right, I go deaf. I can only hear sermons that explicate the day's biblical text. Make it understandable and I'll be grateful and I'll stumble along and figure out on my own how to apply it.

Sometimes, the preacher's message is enthusiastic but unstructured and incoherent like remarks from Sarah Palin. It suggests that seminary courses in preaching – homiletics – teach "just be earnest; everything else follows. You betcha." But it doesn't. Not for me.

The preacher caught in this poor-structure snare (the devil's work, no doubt), and perhaps sensing that things aren't going well, will often whiz right past any number of good stopping places, as if attenuation will make something good of a bad job. I suspect that's an ancient delusion, practiced ever since the church developed the notion that ministers are endowed with divine authority. If your words have that much heft, there's a good chance that the congregation's attention span and bladder control will be of piddling consequence to you.

When encountering such a ministerial mess, I try hard to keep my dissatisfaction from showing.

I like to sit near the front so that the hymn singing comes from behind and wraps around me in a cloud. I love hymns, especially the down-home kind I grew up with, such as "Love Lifted Me" and "Let Your Lower Lights Be Burning" and my mother's favorite, "Brighten the Corner Where You Are." "Down-home" doesn't often find its way into the Anglo-Catholic redoubts where I have worshipped for many years. We're more about the Angelus and incense and processions in which a priest flicks holy water from an aspergillum. The music is mostly plainsong and Renaissance polyphony sung by a professional choir. But not entirely. Now and then, something like "Rock of Ages" makes a guest appearance, and the congregation has a go at it. These are usually rendered in a flaccid, Episcopalian sort of way, and sometimes they are set to funny tunes rarely heard below the Mason-Dixon line, but I welcome their inclusion. They offer a brief trip back to a happy early time in my life.

Sitting where I usually do, I'm plainly visible to the preacher. I don't want to give offense, so I don a serenity mask. I think about St. Stephen, whose face, shortly before he was stoned to death, was reported to have the "look of an angel." I've been disappointed that no one has said to me after church, "Paul, during the sermon, your face had the look of an angel." I guess my acting skills need work.

When the homiletic ride gets rough, thinking about bananas helps smooth the way. I like bananas a good deal more than I like being told how to conduct my life or being subjected to a homily that wouldn't have gotten higher than a C- in any freshman composition class I ever taught.

I suppose we church goers put up with thin-gruel sermons as part of the admission price for receiving the Eucharist; they do feel somewhat like penance. Bad sermons also create a gratifying sense of community. They form a strong bond among us worshippers – like being together in a plane crash except more so, since the experience is repeated fairly often.

Some of my fellow Christians probably find merit and spiritual sustenance in the same sermons that trigger banana thoughts in me. But I expect most people recognize poor preaching when they hear it, even if they don't say so while chatting in the narthex afterward.

I'm particular – one could say rigid – about what constitutes an edible banana. And I'm not alone in that. In fact, I don't recall meeting even one person who would eat any banana other than a perfect one – as usually defined by a personal, easily applied, single criterion.

IN PASSING. SCENES FROM AN UNCONVENTIONAL LIFE

My sister-in-law Robbie will eat only green ones – not a little green either – bright green. Hard enough to drive nails with. My wife Ann, on the other hand, cannot abide a banana that is not in the soft, borderline-squishy state that announces impending banana death. No brown spots, no eat.

I require bananas that fall between these extremes. Nicely yellow. Firm, but not too firm. Two, maybe three, days prior to the appearance of the first brown spot. I know I've gotten the banana quality that the Almighty called me to when I can snap the end off without using a knife. If it's too green, that's not possible. Too ripe is obvious from the spots.

I buy bananas three at a time: one that's yellow but firm for me, one pretty far on its way to banana senescence for Ann, and one of indeterminate maturity that can go either way with the passage of time. Closely observing number three to see how it's turning out can provide a welcome soupçon of diversion for the long-married couple. If they've mislaid the effervescent dialogue that had once been a staple in life with the hottest date either one ever had, they can speculate about how the ripening is going. That's not much, but in a really bad patch, it may get things moving in a better direction.

Another thing about bananas and me. I like to have one every day as part of breakfast. I rarely eat one after 8:00 a.m. That would be an unnatural act. I'm not so inflexible about other breakfast matters. Scrambled eggs can be an OK supper in a pinch. Pizza is an excellent way to start the day. Fried chicken, too. I have fond memories of doing that before I went vegan. I have even – when my fishing buddies insisted – choked down a beer at first light. But bananas are always and only for breakfast. *Selah.*

And another thing. Just one. More than one is, as the Brits say about unthinkable acts, "just not on." *Selah.*

If the sermon happens to be especially long, I turn from rumination on bananas to the mystery of avocado selection. It so happens I have strong avocado juju. If I could, I would describe how it works, but I don't have the words. What is the tactile sensation that tells me an avocado is ready to eat immediately or in a day or two or in a week? I can't say. But I do know. I'm sure I could make good money as a free-lance picker of avocados for supermarket shoppers.

Or apples. The best variety grown in New York State is the Macoun, but it goes soft and mediocre soon after picking. Sometimes when I'm sitting there in the fourth row trying to look like St. Stephen, I turn from thoughts of bananas to firm, juicy Macouns and think about which vendors are more likely to have good ones when I go shopping after church.

The art of watermelon thumping will also serve.

So, thanks to bananas and the like, I'm in a proper Sunday frame of mind when I finally receive Holy Communion, even if it has been preceded by a stillborn homily. Or at least I'm closer to it than I would have been if I'd paid attention.

As the windy Presbyterian preachers of my childhood liked to point out, "The Lord works in mysterious ways, his wonders to perform."

Amen!

Empty Pews. Why They Should Matter to Everyone

Declining membership in mainstream Protestant churches is of a piece with declining membership in service clubs, scouting, masonry, public schools, and other institutions that have long been a unifying force in American life. The respect for authority and tradition and norms that is fundamental to such institutions has come to be viewed as something unnecessary, foolish, or otherwise objectionable. Without that cultural foundation, each of us is left to invent reality, meaning, and personal significance in isolation. And so, we flounder in tribalism, we fear and reject complexity, and we are grievously divided.

Developments in the Episcopal denomination of which I am a member, are typical of changes that bedevil society as a whole.

Mainstream Christian belief and practice have been the ground of my being from birth, but to continue as that person has become challenging. I am far from alone in that. The church has changed so much in the past fifty or so years that many of us who have hung on are glancing at the exit sign.

Besides repellent changes inside the church, we are derided by the growing number of proud seculars on the outside. Too frequently, any statement that touches on faith or related matters is countered by something such as, "I'm not religious" or "I'm spiritual, but I don't care for organized religion." Such positioning implies that we believers have been duped. We aren't being burned at the stake – it's just an annoyance – but I don't like being regarded in this way, especially since these judgmental seculars usually know little or nothing about that thing they are rejecting. They justifiably recoil at fundamentalism, Pat Robertson, and Focus on the Family as simplistic and more political than religious, but then they go on to assume that all Christians are like that. Our detractors are usually ignorant of church history, theology, and the richness of liturgy.

In a whopper of an irony, the more people abandon the mainstream church, the more the church encourages the exodus by misguided efforts to be up-to-date and hip in words and practice. It's the opposite of holding strongly to ancient truths and rituals that are the core of established religion. To be sure, challenges other than liturgical changes exist, but in the main, they were around even when pews were mostly full.

I grew up in a church-every-Sunday Presbyterian family. Not the severe kind, though I wouldn't be surprised to learn that some of my ancestors were close friends of John Calvin.

I was quite comfortable with the way church fit in our life. More than comfortable, actually. It had faults, of course. They ranged from snobbishness to the morally indefensible – Baptists were déclassé, Catholics were abhorrent in ever so many ways, and inclusion of minorities was unthinkable. These were attitudes, not articles of faith, but in my memory they were widespread. (It must be said, however, that the Presbyterianism of my childhood carried the possibility, now largely realized, of overcoming such witless ugliness.)

Objectionable characteristics aside, our religion gave us certainty about who we were, as well as structure for everyday living. It did so by being authoritative without qualification. To be confirmed required memorizing the catechism. Once you'd been drilled on the answers to "What is the chief end of man?" and other fundamental questions, and you said them back to the minister and you were confirmed in the presence of Almighty God and His assembled people, a new life based on premodern absolutes and clear purpose began. At least it did for me.

But in time, I grew tired of the Presbyterian emphasis on preaching. That, and extemporaneous prayers that often went all over the place, sent me looking for something more to my liking.

IN PASSING. SCENES FROM AN UNCONVENTIONAL LIFE

As an undergraduate at the University of Texas, I lived for a time in an ecumenical community. I left it with regret when I found I was unable to be a self-supporting student in an elite liberal arts program and still keep up with the community's reading and lectures on Tillich, Buber, Bonhoeffer, Kierkegaard, and others. A few years later, I tried being a Unitarian. It had some of what I was seeking, and in it, I happened to be the recipient of a singular act of kindness in a time of great need, but it still didn't satisfy.

In the late sixties, I found my way to the Episcopal Church with its elegant liturgy, sense of the sacred, expansive embrace of symbolism and imagery, and elevated artistry in language, music, and movement. In the Mass, the outward forms, the dance steps of the celebrant and acolytes, even some of the hymns were ancient. I liked that. I still do. Singing songs or saying prayers with unnumbered multitudes who had enjoyed them for a thousand years or more is a sure way to experience the presence of God.

I had just begun to learn the structure of the Episcopal liturgy and to memorize the Creed, the Gloria, the General Confession, and other parts of the Mass, when I moved from Austin to Iraq. As different as life was in that place, the liturgy at St. George's Anglican Church in Baghdad was identical in almost every way to that of All Saints Episcopal in Austin. That uniformity became as essential to my religious life as the sense of sharing the pew with all the company of saints from time immemorial.

Upon returning to Austin in 1968, I was dismayed to find that *trial* liturgies were being used. Revision of *The Book of Common Prayer* was afoot. Church leaders wanted the language and outward forms to be more "modern," and in 1979, a new *Book of Common Prayer* was adopted. The 1928 version, which hewed closely to Thomas Cranmer's sixteenth century translation of Latin services, was laid to rest.

The Episcopal church was not alone in modernization of liturgy and practice. It occurred throughout the worldwide Anglican

Communion. Much of mainstream Protestantism joined in. Nowhere was it stronger than in Roman Catholic reforms of Vatican II.

A central argument against the use of traditional language in the Episcopal liturgy goes like this: Thomas Cranmer translated the Latin services to English so that worshippers could understand what was going on. (Vatican II did likewise.) Therefore – big leap here – it's appropriate that the language of the 1928 *Book of Common Prayer* be made more like everyday speech. "I plight thee my troth," for example, must be excised. In 1963, when Ann and I were planning our wedding, our priest told us that "nobody knows what that means." *We* did. And I think most of our friends and family in church that evening did. If they didn't, they would have more or less figured it out, and they certainly would have recognized that what was being said up there by the altar was of inestimable weight. Changing from a foreign language to a known language is not the same as changing from ceremonial language to ordinary language. (A case can even be made for keeping Latin services, so long as they are accompanied by an observed institutional obligation to teach Latin, but that's an argument for another place.)

Except for some deliberate doctrinal alterations, revisionists tend to see changes in wording as merely stylistic. That position overlooks much. Even slight changes of wording involve changes of meaning. "Is now and ever shall be" (1928) is different in small ways and large from "is now and will be forever" (1979), and those who rewrote *The Book of Common Prayer* must surely have recognized this, or they would not have felt the need to make the change. The first phrase suggests inarguable, absolute truth. The tone of the latter is ho-hum appropriate to many occasions, but it serves poorly in solemn religious celebration. One can prefer either form, but to see them as the same is mistaken. "In other words" just does not apply.

The descent into everyday language fails to recognize that it is in the natural order of things for all occasions of moment to employ special-purpose language and movement – the opening of a session of court, military muster, athletic contests, graduation ceremonies, and swearing-in ceremonies. "All rise," salute, put your hand over your heart, "raise your right hand and swear to tell the truth, the whole truth, and nothing but the truth."

The revised language and forms are thought to be not just more understandable but also more inclusive. I suspect revisionists were stung by justified criticism that the Episcopal church was mostly a church of well-off, older white people. So, substitute guitars for plainchant and the pews would fill up with poor people, minorities, and the young. Turn the priest around to face the congregation instead of the altar when he's celebrating Mass. (Never mind that the words of the Mass are directed to God not to those few in the pews.) Change "Confession" to "Sacrament of Reconciliation.") And so on. I'm tempted to ask why those revisionists couldn't have gone down the street and joined some denomination that derived less meaning from solemn ritual, instead of turning rich traditional Episcopal ceremony into something as insipid as the user agreement one signs before downloading some bit of software. But I suppose that would be rude.

It's not just that I personally dislike the changes. More important, the effort has failed to increase membership. Decline continues apace. Besides that, I suspect that changes in the liturgy have excluded as many people as it has brought in.

The current *Book of Common Prayer* offers two different liturgies; Rite I (quasi-traditional language) and Rite II (contemporary language.) Aesthetically, the difference is equivalent to "Taps" being played on a bugle and on a kazoo. To make matters more objectionable, there are alternate forms available at various points within both Rite I and Rite II. Not only that, priests exclude parts of the Mass known as the Ordinary and change the order of service at will. I suppose in time I could get used to a Daily Office and Mass in which Cranmer is but a vague recollection, but I will never get used to not knowing what to expect.

Here's one more weakness in the way we Episcopalians worship these days. Our services require worshippers to read. No longer can we memorize the important parts and recite them by heart the way we say the Pledge of Allegiance or the Boy Scout Oath. Hunting around in a leaflet for the right text and then reading it is an intellectual exercise. Reciting or chanting or singing sacramental statements in chorus is devotional. Besides that, according to numerous sources, around thirty-two million Americans are functionally illiterate. That being the case, dependence on reading in worship is an impediment to Christ's admonition to "go into all the world and preach the gospel to every creature." Just imagine sitting through an Episcopal Mass, if you don't know how to read.

Regrettably, what is going on in mainstream churches is part of a larger cultural shift, an expression of a divisive zeitgeist.

I am not arguing that if my church returned to high ceremony and traditional language and uniform celebrations, it would cause America to become a united people with widespread concern for the common good. But then, because ways of worship are so connected to other aspects of the culture, it would help.

Since I wrote the above, my wife Ann and I have settled in New York City where we are members of Saint Ignatius of Antioch, an Episcopal Church in the Anglo-Catholic tradition. The concerns I have expressed above do not apply to this parish. They continue unaddressed in most Episcopal churches..

Sundays There and Here, Then and Now

When I moved to the Middle East in the 1960s, one of the strongest adjustments I had to make was having Sunday on Friday. For Muslims, Sunday is an ordinary workday; Friday is their holy day. I experienced no day-off-like feelings or religious impulses on Friday. I did have those feelings on Sunday, even though all around me, it was business as usual. Two years in Iraq, Iran, and Jordan, and I never got used to their calendar.

As far back as I can remember, Sunday has always had a special feeling – whether I was working right through it or sleeping off a stupid college hangover or keeping the Sabbath in a traditional Christian way.

The Sunday feeling is a mix; a large measure of restlessness, a same-size portion of calm, and smaller bits of inchoate desire and vague loneliness. When Sunday bedtime arrives, I'm both relieved and regretful. To some degree, it has been this way my whole life. And I'm not especially unusual in this. There is a good deal of scholarship that holds ambivalence and contradictory feelings to be the most notable characteristic of Sundays. See, for example, Craig Harline, *Sunday,* Yale University Press, 2011.

I was brought up in the church, and the Sundays of my childhood followed the Bible-Belt Protestant script. Some of it I liked a lot; some of it, not much. But, in all, from my septuagenarian vantage point today, I'm grateful for the stability of that way of living. There's much to be said for knowing what to expect (especially if you're a child), even if you have reservations about the content of the practice.

In my family, we'd start the day with a slower, bigger breakfast than usual. It often included biscuits, sometimes pork chops – neither of which ever appeared on a weekday. There was no "hurry up, you're going to be late to school," and my dad would not have hurried off to work.

When I lived with my grandparents, brother, and mother during the war, we'd usually be joined by a friend, who didn't get biscuits at home. After he'd had his fill of them at our table, he and my grandfather, a cowboy turned butcher, enjoyed a drink of bourbon. It was my grandfather's only drink of the week. He said it was to combat his cigarette cough. Looking back, I wonder if he winked when he said that. He'd be snoring softly by the time the preacher got even a slight breeze in his sails.

We'd dress in our Sunday best, including, when flowers were blooming, small corsages for the ladies and boutonnieres for men and boys. At church, I liked the hymn singing, didn't care much for the windy extemporaneous prayers, understood little of what the preacher was going on about, and was receptive to the Sunday school lessons. Without fail, I was reassured by a sense of community.

The midday meal was a celebration, and by some mysterious process it was almost ready as soon as we got home from church. I doubt this meal was as agreeable as I recall, but among the recurring events of my childhood, none are recalled more happily than Sunday dinner. Most often, it consisted of pot roast with potatoes and carrots, a salad of iceberg lettuce sprinkled with blue cheese, and many, many glasses of sweet, iced tea. It's clear that fancy cuisine was not what made the meal special. I don't know exactly what did. I suppose it was a combination of things.

It was fundamentally ceremonial, and though at the time I wasn't aware it was a ceremony, I'm pretty sure I liked that about it. Probably everyone likes ceremonies, if they are happy ones, and Sunday dinner at my house always was. We were dressed up. We stayed at the table longer than usual. We used the good dishes and silver. Those things never happened on a weekday.

Oddly, we left out the most common ceremonial marker of Christian meals – we never said grace. I don't know why, and I can't imagine what my parents would have said if I had asked them about it. They met at a meeting of the Christian Endeavor Society, a young people's evangelical organization, and they never slackened in their participation in church life. Nevertheless, the last person in my family I remember offering thanks at family meals was my mother's maternal grandfather. Notwithstanding that missing element, the meal was inextricable from the religious character of the day; it was a follow-on to the morning's church service. The one did not exist without the other.

The afternoon was also scripted, but I didn't like it as much as the earlier part of the day. My parents took a nap. I too may have after I turned twelve and started getting out of bed at 3:30 to throw my paper route. But when I was younger, I was told to "find something to do" and not make noise. Sometimes I'd join a game of H-O-R-S-E at the schoolyard basketball court. Sometimes I'd just ride my bike around looking for friends who were, like me, at loose ends in this weekly absence of structure. It seemed like every kid in the neighborhood was in parentally coerced doldrums.

In late afternoon, the family usually took a drive. I don't know what motivated that; my parents rarely saw anything they weren't already intimately familiar with. Perhaps it was the calmness of it. There was little traffic to annoy them, and they chatted quietly. My brother and I absorbed – not unhappily though with some restlessness – their companionable murmuring about – well, really – about nothing much at all. The mere sound of their voices was reassuring in the same way worshiping with friends and family had been in the morning.

I'm pretty sure the Sunday drive is now extinct. There should have been a ceremony to commemorate the final one. Or at least a note of its passing, such as those that show up from time to time to mark the passing of the last speaker of some language.

Ann recalls the cocktail hour in much the same way. When her father came home from work, he and Ann's mother would sit on the couch and have a drink and chat. Ann was allowed to sit with them

– when very young, with her head in her mother's lap. She could stay only if she did not try to join the conversation. As she recalls it, she sensed that if she did, she would take something dear from all three of them; she was absorbing the comfortable love of two life-mates chatting amiably. To a large extent, it made her the loving and giving person she is now. Parents still have cocktails and talk, but now excluding children from *any* conversation between adults seems to be as extinct as the Sunday drive.

I can't think what we may be substituting these days for languorous moments of inconsequential talk. Certainly not anything that occurs ritually like our Sunday drives or the cocktail hour at Ann's house. Maybe someone will invent an app for it.

After the drive, the curious mix of calm and restlessness continued, maybe even grew a little. We listened to radio shows, such as the *Longines-Wittnauer Hour*. (It may have been on earlier in the afternoon – I don't remember for sure.) Later there were *Fibber McGee*, *Jack Benny*, and other programs.

Supper was invariably leftovers from the big midday dinner or maybe a bowl of cereal or a piece of cheese toast. That's when restlessness became more noticeable; such a supper didn't feel quite right. Then, after a listless stab at homework that I should have done earlier, the once-a-week, special day was over.

This way of having Sunday was typical for observant Protestants, but elements of it were part of everyone's life. In that time (the 1940s and 1950s) and place (small town Texas and Oklahoma), the larger culture had much in common with Protestant practice. So-called blue laws regulated commerce in a way that was intended to keep it consistent with agreed-upon Christian values.

Ann and I once spent a Sunday on the Isle of Harris in Scotland. Harris is a conservative Presbyterian redoubt with a Sunday way of being that could have served as a template for the blue laws I knew growing up. In the morning, we set off with a nearly empty gas tank to

IN PASSING. SCENES FROM AN UNCONVENTIONAL LIFE

drive around and explore the island. We quickly discovered the island to be so bound by Sunday rules that gasoline (and just about everything else) could not be sold then. We had a cold breakfast and a lunch that the proprietress of our B&B had kindly packed for us on Saturday evening. (Cooking was not permitted on Sunday.) And she apologized for not being permitted to do our laundry on Sunday.

After an anxious search for a place to have supper, while the gas gauge dropped ever closer to "empty," we found the one establishment (the hotel) that was serving. Never mind the severity of the Sabbath observance, getting a drink of good whisky (Scottish spelling) was not a problem. In that regard, Sunday on the Isle of Harris was nothing like Sunday in the Bible Belt, where hard liquor by the glass was not available on any day of the week.

In large measure, though, Beaumont Sundays during my childhood were similar to those of Harris. Strictures were less encompassing and less severe, but there was a good deal of regulation of public activities. And for many people, public rules and patterns of personal behavior overlapped.

Most retail establishments were closed. Whether this was by law or by tacit agreement, I don't know. I suspect the latter. Liquor stores, though, were legally prohibited from opening. Television with its broadcasts of morning talk shows and professional sports had not yet arrived. In my recollection, there was relatively little diversion of any sort. The Baptist kids were not even allowed to go to movies on Sunday. It was a day of rest, and rest did not include much that we would recognize today as entertainment. Everything slowed down.

Over the years, I've discontinued the personal Sunday practices of my childhood, but I realized recently that I'd gladly bring back some aspects of the Bible-Belt Sunday – the quiet respite, a script, church attendance, and the big midday meal. For various reasons, it's difficult to continue those traditional ways. Ann and I try, though, and sometimes, if we make judicious substitutions and squint a little, a Sunday in Saranac Lake feels a little like those of my childhood.

I always try not to work – no writing (easy), no household chores (even easier), also no faithless fears and worldly anxieties (not at all easy). Ann joins me in this, though she's Type A through-and-through, and for her, shutting down is rather like closing a nuclear power plant; you don't just turn off the lights and shut the door.

We don't start the day with a bigger-than-usual breakfast, just fruit and bread that Ann has made with jam or peanut butter or butter and honey. But we do have an extra cup of coffee, and we do respond to the elemental urge to slow down and accept the possibility of rest and renewal. We've not found a local church that suits us, so there's no getting dressed up and going to services. Instead, using the Book of Common Prayer, we make our devotions privately and spend more time than usual in quiet deliberation of matters beyond the commonplace. Also, I go to the grocery store at midmorning to get a *New York Times*. When the highway is closed by a winter storm and the paper doesn't get through, we descend into the same sort of withdrawal that accompanies electronic blackout.

On a warm day in summer (which would not be all of them), we take the *Times* and a basket of fruit, sandwiches, and wine and like Ratty and Mole go "messing about" in the pontoon boat. That's similar to the Sunday drive in the way its essence is slow-motion companionship. The chain of lakes is large, so we can usually find an undisturbed cove to anchor in and enjoy the sunshine and read and drink wine and swim naked and take a snooze. We do that occasionally on a weekday, and it's a pleasure, but it isn't the same. It feels kind of like having Sunday on Friday did when I lived in Muslim countries.

Winter Sundays have a less Sabbath-like tone. Conditions permitting, i.e., when the temperature is no lower than ten and the snow is right, we ski at the Olympic cross-country venue. That's far more active than a summer afternoon on the boat, of course, and on its

IN PASSING. SCENES FROM AN UNCONVENTIONAL LIFE

face, it doesn't seem as restful as the ideal Sunday. On the other hand, the trails are so long that, five minutes away from the lodge, we are alone, and it's completely quiet except for the sound of our breathing and the hissing of skis on snow. It's not a worship service, but there is a sense of reverence that is harder to come by on a weekday when we are likely to be in a hurry to get back to some appointment or chore.

Sunday evenings resonate clearly with childhood memories. Often, neither of us wants to cook, so we warm up something from the freezer. *Masterpiece Theatre* stands in for *The Great Gildersleeve*.

Sundays also include porch-sitting in warm weather, sitting by a fire in cold, and catching up on periodicals and the stack of books on the bedside table.

The novelist, Ian McEwan, said in a recent interview that reading poetry involved "taking yourself out of the narrative of daily activity and drawing the neglected cloak of stillness around you." He might just as well have been referring to a proper Sunday.

Don't miss out!

Visit the website below and you can sign up to receive emails whenever PAUL WILLCOTT publishes a new book. There's no charge and no obligation.

https://books2read.com/r/B-A-UYZS-AJWBD

BOOKS 2 READ

Connecting independent readers to independent writers.

Did you love *In Passing. Scenes from an Unconventional Life*? Then you should read *A Franklin Manor Christmas*[1] by PAUL WILLCOTT!

A Franklin Manor Christmas

Paul WIllcott

Annals of Franklin Manor
. Book One [2]

For most potential buyers, Franklin Manor was just a huge run-down old house, a former monastery and tuberculosis sanatorium, half buried in Adirondack snow. But to erstwhile professor, Butch Regent, Franklin Manor was a beacon of hope. It would make his bland and unsatisfactory life meaningful. He would buy it, renovate it, and turn it into an artists' retreat. Lack of money, broken pipes, and pitiless cold almost defeat him but for the help of former patients, angels, a growing group of "temporary" guests, a long-dead altar boy, and a mysterious bell. In the end, the arists' retreat is beginning to take shape – but not in a way Regent recognizes.

---

1. https://books2read.com/u/4D68nk

2. https://books2read.com/u/4D68nk

It's a deep snow, feel-good story in the tradition of *Miracle on Fifth Avenue* and *The Bishop's Wife*.

Read more at paulwillcott.com.

Also by PAUL WILLCOTT

Annals of Franklin Manor
A Franklin Manor Christmas
A Franklin Manor Epiphany

Standalone
12,000 Miles of Road Thoughts. Old Van, Old Man, Recovering Hippie, Dying Cat
In Passing. Scenes from an Unconventional Life

Watch for more at paulwillcott.com.

About the Author

Paul Willcott is a lapsed Texan with four degrees from the University of Texas, including a Ph.D. in applied linguistics and a law degree. He is a retired newspaper columnist, award-winning blogger, novelist, and one-poem poet.

He has lived in Baghdad, Amman, Tehran, London, Hong Kong, Zurich, Washington, D.C., in a former tuberculosis sanatorium/monastery in the Adirondack Mountains, and elsewhere. He and his wife Ann Laemmle are now well settled in New York City.

Read more at paulwillcott.com.

Milton Keynes UK
Ingram Content Group UK Ltd.
UKHW020833141124
451205UK00013B/860